=HOW TO SAVE=
ON YOUR
TAXES
IF YOU MAKE
$30,000
OR LESS

NANCY DUNNAN

PERENNIAL LIBRARY

Harper & Row, Publishers, New York
Cambridge, Philadelphia, San Francisco, London
Mexico City, São Paulo, Singapore, Sydney

This book is sold with the understanding that neither the Author nor the Publisher is engaged in rendering legal or financial services. As each situation is unique, questions relevant to the practice of law or personal finance and specific to the individual should be addressed to a member of those professions to ensure that the situation has been evaluated carefully and appropriately.

The Author and Publisher specifically disclaim any liability, loss, or risk, personal or otherwise, which is incurred as a consequence, directly or indirectly, of the use and application of any of the contents of this work.

FIRST EDITION

Produced by Cloverdale Press, Inc., 133 Fifth Avenue, New York, NY 10003

The author wishes to thank Larry Boxer of Farkouh, Furman & Faccio, New York, NY

Library of Congress Cataloging-in-Publication Data

Dunnan, Nancy.

    How to save on your taxes if you make $30,000 or less.

    1. Tax planning—United States—Popular works. I. Title.

KF6297.Z9D86 1989   343.7304   88-21328
                          347.3034

ISBN 0-06-096321-2 (pbk.)

89 90 91 92 93 FG 10 9 8 7 6 5 4 3 2 1

CONTENTS

Introduction

Overcoming Your Fear of Filing

Tax Reform may or may not mean more dollars in your pocket, but it certainly means more changes—new forms, new calculations, and new confusion. The 1986 Tax Reform Act brought about some 2,700 alterations in the tax code itself, 13 new tax forms, and revisions in 54 old ones. And the revisions are still going on.

All of these changes and the media coverage surrounding them may intimidate you from filling out your own tax return, or even from trying to understand what the Tax Reform Act is all about. But don't worry. If you suffer from fear of filing, you're not alone! Most people are overwhelmed by the number of tax rules and regulations.

How to Save on Your Taxes greatly simplifies the filing process for you. By walking you through your Form 1040, this book will enable you to handle your own return with ease, or at least to discuss it intelligently with a professional tax preparer. Numerous tax-saving tips have been gathered to help you with your particular situation—whether you're a parent, single or divorced, married or widowed, retired or working. You *can* get on top of the situation, save yourself a bundle, and actually wind up giving less to the IRS. And believe it or not, you can minimize the pain and worries that precede April 15.

One reason people shy away from preparing their own tax return or even thinking about their taxes is that the IRS loves to use unusual words. Before going any further, take some time to familiarize yourself with the 24 "IRS-Speak" terms that follow. You don't need to memorize them all, but understanding the IRS jargon will help you feel less intimidated, more knowledgeable, and far better able to evaluate your personal tax situation.

Then you will proceed through Form 1040 line by line, and learn all the right moves to make along the way. Look for the special **TS** symbol, indicating a special "tax-saving" technique that's guaranteed to reduce your payment to the IRS, or boost your refund.

IRS-Speak

Here are 24 of the most popular terms you should understand, and what they mean to the IRS:

Adjusted gross income: Your total taxable income minus certain adjustments, such as contributions to your IRA (Individual Retirement Account) or alimony payments you made to an ex-spouse. Your adjusted gross income (A.G.I.) is entered on the first page of Form 1040. If you do not have any of these adjustments, your A.G.I. is the same as your gross income.

Basis: The total cost of an item, including certain other costs such as legal fees or commissions. For example, the basis of a stock consists of the purchase price plus the stockbroker's commission.

Capital gains or losses: Profits or losses made when an investment, such as real estate or a stock or bond, is sold or exchanged.

Casualty/theft losses: Loss of property or other asset because

2

of an unusual event, such as a flood or fire. Losses are often deductible from your adjusted gross income.

Credit: The dollar amount you can subtract from the income tax you would owe. For example, there is a dollar credit for those age 65 or older. Credits are worth more than deductions because they are subtracted right from the tax you owe, whereas deductions are subtracted from your adjusted gross income.

Deduction: An expense such as mortgage interest or unreimbursed medical bills, which you can subtract from your adjusted gross income. For example, if you're in the 15% tax bracket, $1,000 of unreimbursed medical expenses equals a $150 tax savings.

Dependent: A person whom you financially support and who also meets various tests, therefore entitling you to claim that person as an exemption on your return. Each exemption is worth a specific dollar amount.

Depreciation: An annual deduction you can take when you calculate your income tax for a business asset, such as property, that theoretically loses value with age.

Distribution: A payment of money, such as by a retirement plan to employees or by a trustee or estate to beneficiaries.

Earned income: Money that you earn from your job; money earned from investments is called passive income.

Estimated taxes: Taxes paid four times a year based on your estimate of what your tax liability will be for the year, or on the amount of tax you paid last year. Estimated taxes must be paid if your wage withholding is not enough, or if part of your income, dividends, or interest income is not subject to typical withholding, as is the case with self-employed individuals.

Exemption: An amount you're entitled to deduct from your adjusted gross income before figuring your taxes, based on the number of people you support, including yourself.

F.I.C.A. (Federal Insurance Contribution Act): F.I.C.A. withholdings constitute employee contributions for Social Security coverage.

Floor: The minimum amount that makes a deduction allowable. For example, before you can deduct medical expenses (*i.e.*, itemize them on Schedule A), your total unreimbursed medical expenses must surpass 7.5% of your adjusted gross income. The 7.5% is the floor.

Gross income: Your taxable income from all sources (but not including insurance proceeds, gifts, inheritances, or interest from tax-exempt municipal bonds), before taxes are withheld.

Head of household: An unmarried taxpayer who pays over 50% of the cost of supporting a home for another person for the entire year. That taxpayer is entitled to a lower tax rate than the standard single rate.

Itemizing: Listing all your deductions on Schedule A rather than taking the standard, predetermined deduction. These deductions are then subtracted from your adjusted gross income in order to determine your taxable income.

Joint return: A tax return on which a husband and wife combine their incomes and deductions, to benefit from a lower tax rate than if they filed separately.

Lump-sum distribution: A payment or total of payments made within one tax year of the entire amount due from a qualified pension or profit-sharing plan.

Ordinary income: Income other than that derived from the sale or exchange of a capital asset.

Passive income: Income received from sources such as dividends, interest, royalties, rent, and capital gains—as opposed to income earned actively, such as wages, salary, or tips.

Rollover: A reinvestment of all or part of a distribution made from a company pension plan into a qualified plan of your new employer or into your IRA, within 60 days. A rollover enables you to defer paying taxes on the distribution.

Standard deduction: A predetermined dollar amount that you can deduct from your adjusted gross income if you do not itemize your deductions.

Taxable income: Your income, after subtracting adjustments, deductions, and exemptions. It is the amount on which your tax is computed.

1 Filing: Who, What, and When

Nearly everyone who has some form of income must file a tax return—even some children! But the form that's right for you may not be right for the people next door. The IRS has three basic forms, plus a handful of supplementary Schedules. Your first task is to determine whether or not you need to file. If you do, your next task is to determine the form or combination of forms that's right for you.

Who Must File?

Your personal tax-filing status, your age, and your income determine whether you need to file a tax return.

You must file if you are:	And your 1988 gross income is at least:
Single	
Under age 65 and not blind	$ 4,950
Under age 65 and blind	4,950
Age 65 or older	5,700
Married Filing a Joint Return	8,900
Both under age 65 and neither blind	8,900
Both under age 65 and one or both blind	9,500
Both age 65 or older	10,100
Married Filing a Separate Return	1,950

Head of Household

Under age 65 and not blind	6,350
Under age 65 and blind	6,350
Age 65 or older	7,100

Widow or Widower

Under age 65 and not blind	6,950
Under age 65 and blind	6,950
Age 65 or older	7,550
Married Living Apart	1,950
Nonresident Alien	1,950

There are several other circumstances under which you must file a return:

- If your net (pre-tax) self-employment earnings are $400 or more;

- If you are entitled to a refund (you'll have to calculate your return first to find out);

- If you owe other taxes, such as the alternative minimum tax or an early IRA withdrawal tax;

- If your tax year is less than 12 months—for example, if you started a business in the middle of the year;

- If you are claimed as a dependent on another's return and have either 1) earned income in excess of $3,000; or 2) any investment income at all that is part of a total income of more than $500 (see below).

Children's Taxes

One significant change brought about by the 1986 Tax Reform Act pertains to the tax status of children and other dependents. People who in the past might not have had to file—such as children or others with low incomes—are now obligated to report their income under the provisions of the new tax law.

An individual who can be claimed as another taxpayer's dependent now must file a return if he or she has earned income in excess of $3,000, or if he or she has any investment income at all and a total income of over $500. Dependents who have *no* investment income need not file unless their earned income *exceeds*

6

$3,000 (or unless they have had taxes withheld from earnings which were $3,000 or less, in which case they would be entitled to a refund).

Dependents filing their own returns under these new rules may not take a personal exemption for themselves if they are claimed as a dependent by another taxpayer. They are, however, entitled to a standard deduction that is generally limited to either $500 or the total of their earned income from wages, salary, etc., to the extent of the new standard deduction (usually $3,000)— whichever is greater. If a child under 14 years of age filing his or her own return has investment income, the amount that exceeds $1,000 is taxed to the child at the parent's rate. It may also be necessary to file Form 8615 to compute the tax.

Children old enough to sign their name can sign their own tax return; otherwise, a parent can sign for them.

For more details, read IRS publications #922, "New Tax Rules for Children and Dependents," and #920, "Explanation of the Tax Reform Act of 1986 for Individuals."

When Must You File?

It's April 15 for most of us, but there are a few exceptions:

- If you are a nonresident alien and no taxes were withheld from your wages, you file on June 15;

- If you are a resident alien planning to leave the U.S., you must file no later than 10 days before the date you leave;

- If you report for a fiscal year (if, for example, you are self-employed), your tax return is due on the 15th day of the 4th month after your fiscal year closes;

- If you are self-employed you must file quarterly returns with estimated tax payments. For details, see page 102.

The IRS does not need to *receive* your return by the date it is due, but it must be *postmarked* by midnight of that date. When the due date is a Saturday, Sunday, or a legal holiday, you have until the next business day. (For details on getting an extension—that is, the right to file after your due date—see page 103.)

Which Form Fits?

There are three basic tax forms from which to choose: The easiest is Form 1040EZ, followed by Form 1040A, with Form 1040 the most complex. The 1040 is commonly known as the "long form." The other two are shorter and easier. Select the easiest form, given your income and filing status, as well as the one that permits you to *take all the deductions you possibly can*. The more deductions, the less you pay in taxes. If you are in doubt after reviewing the following material, use the 1040.

1040EZ

Use Form 1040EZ if you meet *all* these requirements:

- Your filing status is single;

- Your taxable income is under $50,000;

- You do not itemize your deductions;

- You do not qualify for the additional deduction for being over age 65 or being blind;

- You do not claim a deduction for dependents;

- Your income is derived solely from wages, salaries, and tips, and your interest income is less than $400;

- You do not claim any tax credits.

1040A

Use Form 1040A if you meet *all* these requirements:

- Your taxable income is less than $50,000;

- You do not itemize your deductions;

- Your income is derived only from wages, salaries, tips, interest dividends, or unemployment compensation;

- Your only deduction is for an IRA contribution;

- Your only credits are for child care and dependent-care expenses and/or earned income.

1040

Use Form 1040 if you itemize your deductions or if you claim deductions or credits not listed as part of the previous two forms. You *must* file the 1040 if you meet *any* of these requirements:

- Your taxable income is above $50,000;

- You itemize your deductions;

- You had income other than wages, salary, tips, unemployment compensation, interest, or dividends—such as income derived from barter, a pension or annuity, a property sale, alimony, self-employment;

- You receive taxable Social Security benefits or railroad retirement benefits;

- You receive interest on securities sold between interest payment dates (for example, when you sell bonds you must report the amount of interest they have accrued, even though you did not actually receive it);

- You receive nontaxable dividends;

- You receive capital-gains distributions (for example, from a mutual fund or sale of stock);

- You receive foreign earned income;

- You and your spouse file separate returns, and your spouse itemizes deductions;

- You file as a widow or widower;

- You claim adjustments to your return, such as alimony or payments to a Keogh retirement plan;

- You made estimated tax payments during the year;

- You sold your house (whether at a profit or a loss);

- You received $20 or more in tips during any one month and you did not report them in full to your employer;

- You claim a tax credit other than for child and dependent care or for the earned income credit, such as a credit for the elderly or permanently disabled;

- You are liable for other types of taxes, such as the Alternative Minimum Tax (AMT) or self-employment tax (you must calculate your taxes first to determine if you are indeed liable).

2 Your Filing Status

Now that you've determined you must file a return and you've selected the appropriate IRS form, you're ready to select the right filing status. The five statuses are described below. Read through all of them and then select the one that is both appropriate and financially most advantageous.

Lines 1 through 5 on Form 1040 all deal with your filing status. Choosing the correct status is an important factor in reducing your tax bite, because it determines the tax rate you pay as well as the dollar amount of your standard deduction. It also affects whether you can take other deductions or credits. The five categories are:

1) Single

2) Married Filing Jointly

3) Married Filing Separately

4) Head of Houshold

5) Widow or Widower

You must check one of these five categories on Form 1040.

Generally, the lowest rates are for married filing jointly, while married filing separately tend to pay the highest (see **TS** below).

When to File Singly   Line 1

As far as the IRS is concerned, your marital status for the year is determined by your marital status on the last day of the calendar year. Therefore, you are single for your 1988 return if you were not married on December 31, 1988. Even if your legal separation or divorce only became effective on that day, you are regarded as

10

single for the entire year and must file as a single, unless you qualify for Head of Household status (see box below).

> (TS) Singles who provide support for dependents may qualify as head of household, and as such pay taxes at a lower rate than other singles. (See pages 13–14 for details.)

Married: Joint Filing or Separate Filing?

The 1986 Tax Reform Act has led to a great many more couples splitting up—their tax forms, that is. In the past, two-income couples were generally better off filing jointly, but what worked in the past may no longer be the answer today. It's true, tax rates are still lower for those who file jointly, but some other rules, explained below, mean some couples are better off filing separately.

For example, a key reason for marrieds to consider filing separately is that the percentage "floor"—the amount you need in order to declare certain deductions—has been increased. Since this amount is based on the income shown on a return, it is usually more difficult for two-income couples to meet this floor on a joint return than it is for a single or for marrieds filing separately.

(**Note:** The best break for those filing jointly—the two wage-earner deduction—was eliminated by the 1986 Tax Reform Act. It allowed married couples to subtract 10% of the income of the spouse who earned less—up to $3,000—from their combined adjusted gross income.)

• **If you receive Social Security,** filing separately may be a disadvantage. For married couples filing separately, 50% of their Social Security payments are taxed regardless of income. But if they file jointly, they do not pay taxes on Social Security unless 50% of their Social Security payments, *plus* their other income, including tax-exempt interest, exceeds $32,000.

• **If you manage real estate,** filing separately may be a disadvantage. With a joint return, couples who own and actively manage real estate are entitled to $25,000 of "passive" losses from rental income that can be used to offset their regular salary and dividend income. When filing separately they miss out on this savings, unless they have not lived together at all during the year. (See page 80 for details.)

• **Miscellaneous expenses**—such as unreimbursed employee business expenses, investment advisory fees, safe-deposit box rental costs, and tax-preparation fees—are still deductible, but *only* when they exceed 2% of your adjusted gross income (previously these expenses were fully deductible). Therefore, if one spouse paid a sizable amount in investment expenses, filing a separate form may be best because that spouse, on his or her own, may be able to exceed this 2% floor. It is obviously more difficult to exceed 2% when you're dealing with combined incomes.

• **Unreimbursed medical expenses** are governed by a similar ruling: You can deduct only those unreimbursed expenses that exceed 7.5% of your adjusted gross income.

 If most of your medical expenses belong to one spouse, then it may pay to file separately in order to meet the new higher percentages.

• **Your IRA (Individual Retirement Account)** status might also be improved by filing separately. A spouse who is not covered by a retirement plan at work can claim an IRA deduction when filing separately, even if the other spouse is covered at work— provided that the non-covered spouse has an adjusted gross income of less than $10,000. If a married couple has a combined adjusted gross income of between $40,000 and $50,000 and one has an employer-sponsored plan, then only a partial IRA deduction is allowed if they file jointly. No deduction is allowed if the adjusted gross income is $50,000 or more on a joint return. The spouse who has an employer plan may claim a partial IRA deduction *only* if the adjusted gross income is less than $10,000, and may take no deduction if it is $10,000 or more.

• **State taxes may offer a saving,** depending on where you live. Several states, including California and New York, require couples who file jointly to pay state taxes jointly as well. At the same time, they've lowered rates for couples filing separately.

> (TS) State income taxes are still deductible from your federal return, whether you file jointly or separately.

When to File Jointly   Line 2

If you are married you can file either jointly with your spouse, or separately. If you elect joint filing, then all income, deductions, and credits for both of you are combined. Filing jointly usually saves on taxes because the rates are lower.

When to File Separately   Line 3

If you and your spouse file separately, each of you reports his or her own income, deductions, and credits. There are some major disadvantages to filing separately: the rates are higher, and you cannot claim certain credits, such as the child-care credit. Rental property deductions and tax-free Social Security benefits are also eliminated or reduced. It also means you both must itemize, or you both must take the standard deduction.

When to File
as Head of Household   Line 4

If you're single, try to file as head of household; you will pay less tax than if you file simply as a single. If you are a single parent, or are supporting one or both of your own parents, you may qualify. To be a head of household:

1) You must be unmarried, legally separated, divorced with a final court decree, or married but living apart from your spouse with a separate maintenance agreement (see page 14).

2) You must pay over half the qualifiable costs of keeping up a

13

home for the taxable year. These costs include: rent, mortgage interest, taxes, insurance, repairs, utilities, domestic help, and food eaten at home. They do *not* include clothing, education, medical care, trips, vacations, or transportation.

3) The house must be your primary residence, with the exception that applies to housing for your parents as explained in the tax-saver box below.

4) This home must also be the principal home of "a relative" for more than 6 months of the taxable year (see box on page 15 for a list of relatives). The relative generally must be a dependent (see pages 16–20); an unmarried child, stepchild, adopted child, or grandchild does not have to be your dependent.

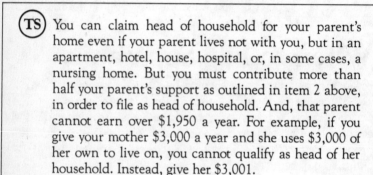

(TS) You can claim head of household for your parent's home even if your parent lives not with you, but in an apartment, hotel, house, hospital, or, in some cases, a nursing home. But you must contribute more than half your parent's support as outlined in item 2 above, in order to file as head of household. And, that parent cannot earn over $1,950 a year. For example, if you give your mother $3,000 a year and she uses $3,000 of her own to live on, you cannot qualify as head of her household. Instead, give her $3,001.

Head of Household and Married

There is one situation in which you can be married and still file as head of household—if you're married but living apart from your spouse. But you must meet all these conditions:

1) You must file a separate return.

2) You must pay over half the cost of maintaining your home.

3) Your spouse must not have lived with you during the year.

4) Your home must have been the main residence for over 6 months of the year for your *child or stepchild*, whom in this case you must be able to claim as a *dependent*.

WHO IS A RELATIVE?

- Child, stepchild, adopted child
- Grandchild, great-grandchild
- Mother, father, stepmother, stepfather
- Grandparent, great-grandparent
- Sister, brother, half sister, half brother, stepsister, stepbrother
- Mother-in-law, father-in-law, daughter-in-law, son-in-law, sister-in-law, brother-in-law
- Aunt, uncle, niece, nephew (but only if related by blood)

When to File as Widow or Widower   Line 5

You can generally reduce your taxes if you file a joint return. But if you are widowed and meet *all* five of the requirements listed below—the most important being that you have a dependent child living with you—you can still file a joint return, and reap the benefits of lower rates.

1) Your spouse must have died within the two years prior to the tax year for which you are filing (for example, if your spouse died in 1986, you can file as a widow or widower for tax years 1987 and 1988; you may file a joint return for the year of his or her death).

2) You could have filed a joint return the year your spouse died, although you need not actually have done so.

3) You did not remarry before the end of the tax year for which you are filing.

4) You have a dependent child who lived with you during the tax year for which you are filing and for whom you can claim an exemption.

5) You must have paid more than half of the costs of keeping up your home for all of the tax year for which you are filing.

3 Exemptions

Now that you've determined your tax filing status, you're ready to deal with Line 6—personal exemptions. A personal exemption is a preset dollar amount you can deduct from your income *before* you calculate your tax. You deduct this amount for every qualified person you financially support, including yourself. Although a person can be declared an exemption for only one taxpayer, those declaring exemptions often can declare more than one person.

 Declare as many exemptions as you can; each one is worth $1,950 in tax year 1988; $2,000 in tax year 1989.

Who Qualifies as an Exemption?

You can claim exemptions for:

• **Yourself.** Every taxpayer has this one exemption, unless, of course, you're the dependent of another taxpayer and are being claimed by that person. For example, if your parents can claim you as an exemption, you cannot claim an exemption for yourself. And, even if you are claimed as someone else's exemption, if you have income or are entitled to a refund you must still file a return—on which you *cannot* claim yourself as an exemption.

• **Your husband or wife.** You may also claim your spouse in addition to yourself. But, if your spouse has any gross income at all, you must file a joint return in order to claim your spouse. If he or she does *not* have gross income and is *not* a dependent of another taxpayer, and you file a separate return, you can still claim your spouse on your separate return. Your spouse would not then claim himself or herself on his or her return.

• **Your children and other dependents.** The IRS does not limit the number of dependents you can claim. However, in order to claim any dependents, conditions in *all* five of these qualifying categories must be met: 1) relationship (or member of household); 2) support; 3) income; 4) citizenship or residency; and 5) for married dependents, no joint return.

Relationship Test

Your dependent must live in your house for the full year, *unless* he or she is related to you (see box on page 15). Also, any person, related or not, who made your home his or her principal residence for the full year *and* whom you supported, such as a friend, foster child, or cousin, passes the relationship test. If your dependent was either born or died during the year, the relationship test is met if he or she lived in your household while alive.

 If you have a foster child who lived with you for the full year, you can claim an exemption for him or her. A foster child can be considered a dependent if your home is his or her principal residence for the year.

Note: For tax purposes, relationships that are the result of your marriage (as opposed to blood relationships) need not end with either the death of, or your divorce from, your spouse. Your stepchild can still be a dependent stepchild even after your husband or wife—his or her father or mother—dies, or if you divorce his or her parent: If the five tests are met, the stepchild can be claimed as a dependent.

Support Test

To meet the support test, you must provide more than half of your dependent's total support. You must be able to prove the expenditures, although only certain ones qualify. If they are in the form of "property" (such as food, clothing, or housing), use their fair market value—*i.e.*, calculate what a stranger would pay and use that figure.

These items, if you provide them for your dependent, count toward support:

- Fair rental value of a room, apartment, or house (if the dependent lives in his or her own home and you help contribute to items including mortgage interest payments, real estate taxes, or repairs, reduce the total fair rental value of the home by the amount you contribute);

- Cost of clothing, food, education, medical and dental services (including insurance payments);

- Recreation (things like lessons or summer camp);

- Transportation;

- Wedding clothes and reception for a dependent;

- Dependent care expenses (babysitter, nursery school).

The following do not count toward support:

- A dependent's life insurance premiums;

- Funeral expenses for the death of a dependent.

Multiple Support Agreements

A multiple support agreement is a viable technique for reducing your taxes: If you and someone else provide support for a dependent but neither of you can meet the 50% support test, then investigate a multiple support agreement—assign the dependent's exemption to one or the other of you; then change the agreement each year so that you alternate claiming the exemption. To set up such an agreement, you must provide more than 10% of the person's total support, and the total amount contributed by you and the others must equal more than half the support. Those waiving their rights to claim the exemption must fill out Form 2120, the "Multiple Support Declaration."

For example, you, your sister, your brother, and your stepsister all help support your mother, who lives in her own apartment. You and your brother each provide 40%, your sister and stepsister, 10%

each. None of you meets the 50% requirement. Your brother waives his right this year so you can take the exemption, with the understanding that he will take it next year. Your sisters do not qualify at all since neither provides more than 10% of your mother's support.

For Custodial Parents

If you are a divorced or separated parent and are regarded as the custodial parent, and if you do not have a multiple support agreement such as the one described above, then you automatically qualify for the support test if you meet all of these requirements:

1) You are divorced, legally separated, or lived apart from your spouse at all times during the last 6 months of the year;

2) One or both parents (as opposed to a grandparent or another relative) provide more than 50% of the child's total support for the year;

3) One or both parents have custody of the child for more than half the year;

4) The child's support is not governed by a multiple support agreement.

> **(TS)** Remember, only one person can take the exemption. But even if you are not the custodial parent, *you* still might qualify for the exemption if the custodial parent agrees and signs a written agreement to that effect— Form 8332, "Release of Claim to Exemption for Child of Divorced or Separated Parents." Indicate on the waiver if it is applicable for one year or longer.

Income Test

Your dependent cannot have more than $1,950 worth of gross income annually, exclusive of nontaxable income. There is one exception to this rule: a dependent who is under age 19 or who is a full-time student for 5 months of the year has no cap placed on his or her income. For example, your stepson graduated from college in June and then went on to law school in September. Although he earned $3,500 during the summer, you can still claim him as a dependent since he was a full-time student for at least 5 months of the year.

Citizenship Test

A dependent must be a citizen or resident of the U.S., or a national or resident of Canada or Mexico. You cannot claim a foreign-exchange student who lives with you. (A national is one who owes permanent allegiance to the U.S.—generally a person born in American Samoa who has not become a naturalized American citizen.)

 If you hosted a foreign-exchange student, you may be able to take a charitable deduction for the unreimbursed expenses you incurred for the student's care. Check with a tax professional for details.

Joint Return Test

A married person can qualify as a dependent of someone other than his or her spouse, but only if he or she has a gross income of less than $1,950 and does not file a joint tax return—unless the only purpose of filing the joint return is to claim a refund.

Once you have determined who your dependents are, multiply the number of dependents times $1,950 and enter it on Line 36 of Form 1040. Then deduct this amount from your total income. Be sure to supply Social Security numbers for all dependents aged 5 years or older.

Remember: If you claim a child as a dependent, that child can no longer use the personal exemption for himself or herself on a return he or she files.

4 | Income

T he one question that haunts all of us is whether our income is taxable. The answer, unfortunately, is almost always a resounding "yes." In fact, the IRS definition of income is far broader than you might think and includes much more than your wages, salary, dividends, and interest income. It encompasses such diverse sources as game-show prizes, refunds of state and local income taxes that you deducted the prior year (a refund of federal income tax is not taxable), winnings at a casino, and even some Social Security benefits, much to the dismay of retired people. Yet, there are exceptions—income you do *not* need to report. There are also ways of handling your income that will defer or reduce taxes.

What You Must Report

It's important to understand what truly constitutes income, because the amount of tax you end up paying is actually based on a percentage of your income. And, if you inadvertently neglect to include any taxable income on your return, the IRS will ultimately charge you a penalty and interest on the additional tax due. (Check the following list of all taxable income.)

TAXABLE INCOME ITEMS

- Alimony
- Annuities: Depending on the plan, a portion may be taxed
- Barter income: If the goods or services you receive are worth more than those you give
- Board of directors' fees

21

- Bonuses
- Business income
- Commissions
- Court awards or damages (but not if for personal injury, libel, or slander)
- Death benefits in excess of $5,000 from a deceased employee's annuity, paid to you
- Disability (if payments replace lost income and premiums were paid by employer)
- Distributions from your IRA
- Endowments
- Farm income
- Fees (for services and for property received as payment for services instead of cash)
- Foreign income above a certain figure (usually $70,000)
- Gambling winnings
- Illegal income
- Jury pay
- Life insurance premiums paid by employer in excess of the group limit
- Military pay
- Moving expenses (reimbursement)
- Notary fees
- Pension and profit-sharing-plan distributions: Depending on the plan, a portion may be taxed
- Prizes and awards
- Rental income
- Salary
- Severance pay

- Social Security benefits: Depending on other income, a portion may be taxable

- Strike benefits (unless they are made to union *and* non-union members alike and are based on individual needs)

- Tips

- Trust and estate income

- Trustee's commissions

- Unemployment compensation

- Vacation pay

- Wages

- Zero coupon bonds: Yearly increases in value, considered but not paid out as interest

The Main Sources of Taxable Income

Although the government considers numerous items taxable income, most of us receive our income from just one or two of them. Five main sources are described in greater detail below. (Interest and dividend income are covered in Chapter 5.)

Wages, Salaries, and Tips

Wages, salaries, tips, bonuses, awards, commissions, and severance pay are all taxable, and are reported on Line 7 of Form 1040. Royalties are taxable also and are reported on Line 18. Bonuses are taxable, even if they are given as gift certificates.

If you are employed, your taxable compensation is given in Box 10 of the W-2 form you receive from each of your employers. If you are self-employed, if you are the sole proprietor of a business, or if you receive income as an independent contractor, then you must report your income on Schedule C, Business Income. There are other circumstances in which you must file Schedule C even if you receive earnings reported on Line 7: if you freelance, if you have a part-time business, or if you do consulting work.

Payment in Property

Payment in property, rather than in cash, must be reported; give the fair market value of the property, which could be, for example, an automobile, shares of stock in your employer's company, a product made by the company you work for, or the like. (Gifts having a value under $25—a Thanksgiving turkey, for example, or a ticket to a ball game—are not taxed.) If your employer lets you buy property or stock from the company at less than fair market value, you must report the difference as income.

Tips

If you receive tips of more than $20 per month while working for any one employer, you must either: 1) inform your employer in writing of the amount of tips you have received and will report to the IRS, or 2) file Form 4070, "Employee's Report of Tips to Employer." You must report to your employer by the 10th day following the month in which you received the tips. Your employer will withhold the Social Security and income tax due on the tips either from your wages or from funds you give him or her for that specific purpose.

(TS) If you work for two or more different employers—bartending at parties, for example—and you get $15 in tips from one and $18 from another, you don't need to report the $33 to any employer because you received less than $20 from each one. No formal paper work is required between you and your employer for tips of less than $20; however, you must report the $33 on your tax return.

The IRS assumes that in large restaurants or cocktail lounges where more than 10 people work, employees pool their tips and then each receives 8% of the restaurant's gross receipts as tips.

If you receive a substantial amount of money in tips, you should keep adequate records. Record them daily in a diary, indicating the date, place, hours worked, and amount of tips received. The IRS Form 4070A is designed for this purpose. Keep your records for three years after filing: The IRS has been known to audit cab drivers, skycaps, and others and prove that they have underreported their tips.

Business Income   Line 12

If you are a sole proprietor of a business you must file Schedule C for reporting your income. (This category is not for those whose business is set up as a corporation, partnership, or joint venture.) Sole proprietorship income could include, for example, income by owners of a business, or self-employed professionals such as accountants, lawyers, doctors, free-lance writers, artists, or consultants. You must attach Schedule C whether this is your only line of work, or it represents work in addition to your regular job. If you have more than one sole proprietorship, you must file a separate Schedule C for each business.

 It is advantageous to file Schedule C because it allows you to subtract all business deductions from your business income without having to meet the 2% floor for miscellaneous deductions.

Unemployment Compensation   Line 20

It may not seem fair, but unemployment compensation is regarded as a form of income by the IRS—whether it's from the government or a company-financed fund. No taxes are withheld from unemployment checks when you receive them, but you must ultimately pay tax on unemployment compensation as you would on regular wages.

 Strike benefits are not always treated as income. They are treated as a nontaxable gift if: 1) the union gives the benefits to all strikers, even non-union people; 2) the union does not insist that you picket; and 3) the benefits are based on need. Consult your union official for more details.

Disability Income Line 7 or 17

If your employer paid for your disability coverage, then your disability payments are taxable. If these payments are included in your wages and are reported on your W-2, they will be part of the income you report on Line 7. If disability payments are part of a pension, report them on Line 17.

Worker's Compensation Line 7

These payments are generally not taxed. However, in certain instances a portion of worker's compensation payments are taxed. Discuss the details with your employer if you are going to receive worker's compensation.

NONTAXABLE ITEMS

- Accident insurance (employer contributions)

- Business gifts with a value of less than $25

- Child support

- Company car: The value of a car used for business only is not taxed.

- Court awards or damages (from a personal injury, libel or slander lawsuit)

- Disability income, other than for loss of wages

- Discounts (value of goods or services you purchase from your employer as a fringe benefit)

- Dividends (originally issued in the form of shares of stocks; cash dividends are taxed, however)

- Employee benefits (such as meals and lodging provided for employer's benefit)

- Foreign income (up to $70,000 earned from a foreign employer while working abroad)

- Foster care payments (for foster individuals who live in your home)

26

- Free parking (value of, if at or near work)

- Health insurance (employer contributions)

- Health insurance: reimbursement for medical or dental expenses you incurred

- Housing (if on certain business premises, such as schools and hospitals)

- Inheritances, up to a certain amount: This is a complicated area, and the rules change frequently, so check with your accountant.

- Interest income on certain state and municipal bonds (check with your broker or accountant)

- Job interview expense reimbursements

- Life insurance (buildup of cash or loan value)

- Life insurance (employer contributions on the first $50,000 of term policies if all employees receive the same benefits)

- Life insurance (proceeds you receive as beneficiary)

- Loans (repayment to you of the principal loans you've made to others)

- Meals (value of, if furnished on the employer's business premises)

- Medical expenses (insurance reimbursements for non-deductible items)

- Pension plans (employer contributions to qualified plans, such as 401[K])

- Scholarships (for tuition, books, supplies—but not for housing and meals—if you're working for a degree)

- Social Security benefits: Depending on other income, a portion may be nontaxable.

- Strike benefits (but only if made to union and non-union workers alike and based on need)

- Subscriptions (value of work-related periodicals paid for by your employer)

- Tuition: If your employer pays for job-related courses, you are not taxed on the dollar amount.

- Veterans' benefits and dividends on veterans' life insurance

- Welfare payments

- Worker's compensation (for job-related injuries or illnesses)

The Main Sources of Nontaxable Income

Check through the list below (as well as the list of taxable items on pages 21–23) before you report anything as income.

Fringe Benefits

Not everything your employer gives you is taxed as income. These items are not taxed:

1) "No-additional-cost" services that are sold to regular customers but given free to employees, such as free flights for airline employees, are untaxed.

2) You don't have to pay tax on the value of discounts that you take advantage of, such as a 15% discount on store merchandise if you are an employee of the store.

3) The value of property or services that would be deductible if you paid for them, such as a car provided by your employer solely for your business use, is untaxed. (As a rule, you are better off getting something free than paying for it and then deducting it.)

4) No tax is paid on the cost of minimal-value items, such as free coffee, personal letters typed at the office, or service pins.

5) The cost of meals and lodging provided for the employer's convenience is tax-free. This typically occurs because an employee works so far from eating facilities that he or she could not leave and get back in a reasonable amount of time, or because of a short lunch period or the need to work through the lunch hour. Waiters, hospital personnel, and bank tellers, for example, often get these kinds of benefits. This applies only if, in the case of meals, they are furnished on the employer's business premises; and if, in the case of lodging, the employee is required to accept the lodging as a condition of employment. Cash reimbursements for meal expenses, however, are included in gross income.

6) The value of campus housing for employees of an educational institution is not taxed when adequate rent is charged. If this situation applies to you, check with your employer or an accountant. Each situation varies.

7) The rental value of a house for an ordained minister is tax-exempt, as is the amount of a rental allowance, as long as the allowance is actually used to pay rent.

8) Lodging for domestic employees or hotel personnel is not taxed. If you work as a domestic, and live in, the value of your room is nontaxable. The same is true for a hotel manager who lives in a hotel.

9) Contributions made by your employer for health and accident insurance premiums, and premiums on the first $50,000 per person of group term life insurance if all employees receive the same level of coverage, are not taxed.

10) Contributions made by your employer to qualified pension and profit-sharing plans, and to some legal services, educational assistance, and dependent care plans are tax-free (check with your employer for details).

Worker's Compensation

Payments made from a state fund to someone injured while on the job are not taxed. But if you return to your job, do only light work, and continue to receive payment in addition to your salary, the compensation payments are taxable. (Check with your accountant, employer, union, or state agency about disability insurance and payments—the rules are complicated and vary widely.)

Military Pay

Although military pay is generally taxable, you may be able to exclude from taxation any reimbursements you receive for moving if the move is service-connected, for overseas living costs, for family separation, and for other allowances. There are other tax-exempt benefits offered to military personnel, such as housing and cost-of-living allowances to cover excess costs. However, these depend on one's position in the organization and on other variables; the government notifies military personnel individually regarding the tax status of such items.

Veterans' Benefits

These are not taxed as long as they fall under laws administered by the Veterans Administration. Tax-free items include pension payments and other benefits for the disabled, subsistence allowances, and educational and training expenses.

5 Interest Income

The basic guideline to keep in mind about interest is that it is nearly always taxable; the exception is interest earned on the majority of state and municipal bonds. Interest income is generally reported in the year in which it is received, although there are exceptions. It is reported on Line 8 of Form 1040, and if your interest income for the year is over $400, you will need to fill out Schedule B. If your interest income is derived from your bank account, or from a "NOW" (interest-bearing checking) or similar account, the bank will send you and the IRS Form 1099-INT showing the total amount of interest you earned. Make certain this dollar amount agrees with your records. The IRS checks what you report against the amount on Form 1099-INT.

At Your Bank

There was a time when the only interest-bearing vehicle a bank had to offer was a traditional passbook savings account. Not any longer, of course—today's saver has a wide variety of options from which to choose. No matter what the source of your bank interest, however, it will be taxed.

Savings Accounts
You must report all interest earned during the year, even if you do not present your passbook to have interest entered, or even if you do not withdraw the interest. Some institutions, such as credit unions and savings banks, pay what are called dividends on interest-bearing accounts; these, too, are taxed as interest income.

Certificates of Deposit
The way you handle CD interest depends on the maturity of the certificate and when you cash it in.

1) Interest earned on a CD that matures the same year you buy it (a CD of less than 1 year) is credited that year and taxable that year.

2) With a CD that matures in 1 full year or less, you can defer taxes: If it is taken out in one calendar year but actually matures in the next, interest is not taxable until the year it matures. For example, you take out a 6-month CD on September 15, 1988; it matures on March 15, 1989. Interest is credited at maturity and is taxable in 1989.

3) If a CD matures in one year or more, interest is said to be earned monthly and you must pay taxes on the amount earned each individual year. For example, you take out a 2-year CD on September 15, 1988. It comes due September 15, 1990. You will have earned interest in 1988, in 1989, and in 1990. You must pay taxes in all 3 years.

 If you redeem a CD early and therefore pay a penalty, you may deduct that penalty on Line 28 of Form 1040, even if you do not itemize.

Gifts
If you receive a free gift for opening a bank account, the fair market value is regarded as taxable income. For example, if you receive a book worth $10 and your account earns $200 in interest,

your Form 1099-INT will note $210 in interest income for that year.

Who Pays the Tax?

If you have bank accounts held in two names (yours with someone else's), it can affect your tax situation. If you are married and file jointly, you must report all joint bank interest on your joint return. But if the account is held in your name and that of someone other than your spouse, the interest income is taxable to the person whose Social Security number is on the account. If two Social Security numbers are listed, then the person whose name and number are listed first is generally the one who will be taxed.

If you have such a joint account, yours is the only or the first Social Security number listed, and you receive the Form 1099-INT, you can file a "nominee" form (Form 1096, "Annual Summary and Transmittal of U.S. Information Returns") with your tax return in order to report that half of the income belongs to the other person.

If you fail to report all interest income, the IRS may bill you for the tax you owe, the interest, and a 5% penalty. If you are questioned, write to the IRS explaining that half of the interest was reported on the return of another person.

U.S. Savings Bonds

Savings bonds provide a unique form of tax shelter—that is, you're not required to pay tax on the interest they earn until they mature or you cash them in prior to maturity. (You can elect to pay taxes on savings bonds annually to avoid a lump-sum payment, but very few people do.)

Series EE Savings Bonds

The most popular savings bonds are Series EE bonds, which are sold in denominations ranging from $50 to $10,000. EE savings bonds sell at a 50% discount of their face value; therefore, a $50 EE bond costs $25.

The $25 difference between the purchase price of $25 and the full face value of $50 represents the interest. And, as noted above, interest is taxed only when the bonds reach maturity and are redeemed, or when they are cashed in before maturity.

Series HH Bonds

These are issued at full face value and pay a fixed rate of interest. They range in denomination from $500 to $10,000. Interest on these bonds is paid every 6 months, and you must pay tax in the year the interest is received.

Rolling Over Series EE's into Series HH's

When your EE bonds mature you can continue to defer taxes due on them by rolling them over into Series HH bonds. When you do this, the face of the new HH bond is stamped to indicate that it includes so many dollars' worth of deferred EE interest. You will not be taxed on this deferred interest until these HH bonds mature or are redeemed.

Who Pays the Tax?

Savings bonds are often held in the names of two people, particularly when they are given as gifts. Bear in mind that the tax on the interest will be paid by the person whose Social Security number appears on the bond. If you are buying bonds for your children, grandchildren, or anyone else, give their Social Security number so they will be the owner of the bond and therefore responsible for the tax. If you don't know what their number is, or they don't have one, you can still purchase the bond in both your names with your Social Security number, defer the taxes until you find out your co-owner's Social Security number, or until they obtain one, and then transfer ownership.

Changing Owners

Savings bonds cannot be sold, but they can be *assigned* to another person by surrendering the bond and having it reissued in the new owner's name. If you were the one who initially purchased the bond, you are taxed for all the interest earned up until the transfer date, at which time the new owner takes over.

Treasury Bills

"T-bills," like savings bonds, are sold at a discount, although unlike savings bonds the discounts vary widely. They mature in anywhere from 90 days to 1 year. When you redeem them at maturity, the difference between the discount price you paid and the full face value represents the interest, which is taxable in the year you redeem the bills. If you sell your T-bill at a gain prior to maturity, your gain consists of interest income and excess capital gain. Both are subject only to federal tax.

Corporate Bonds

Most corporate bonds are issued at face value and pay interest twice a year. The tax on the interest is due when you receive it. If you buy or sell bonds between interest dates, part of the sale price represents the accrued interest. That part is taxable as interest income to the seller and is a separate tax item from any price gain or loss you incur. (Price gains or losses are known as capital gains or losses and are reported on Line 13.)

Zero Coupon Bonds

These bonds, which are known as OID's, for "Original Issued Discount," sell at a deep discount from face value and do not pay annual interest. Upon maturity you receive the full face value. The difference between the full face value and the purchase price is considered the interest. Even though you do not collect this "interest," the IRS requires that you report it as if you had received it. In other words, the annual increase in the value of the bond is treated as taxable income and is reported to you on Form 1099-OID, "Statement for Recipients of Original Issue Discount."

 Zeros are best invested in an IRA or pension plan where taxes are deferred, or for those who will pay low or no taxes.

Market Discount

With the exception of zero coupon bonds, most other bonds are initially issued at or near face value; afterward they trade publicly, rising and falling in price based on the strength of the issuer, on economic conditions, and on the direction of interest rates. If you

buy a bond in the "secondary" or "after" market at a discount—
i.e., at less than face value—it could be subject to "market
discount" rules. In this case, the gain you make when you sell the
bond is treated as interest income and not as capital gain. Check
the instructions in IRS publication #550, "Investment Income and
Expenses," regarding your particular investment.

Other Types of Interest

These five types of interest income are all taxable:

1) Interest on the federal, state, or local tax refund that you
deducted in the prior year. (If you filed for a refund, the IRS will
pay interest on the refund if it fails to pay the refund by 45 days
after the due date of the return, or the date that your return was
filed, whichever is later.)

2) Interest on condemnation awards. (Condemnation refers to
the taking of private property by federal, state, or local governments for public use, in return for compensation.)

3) Interest on payments on seller-financed sales.

4) Interest on certain savings and loan, credit union, or other
accounts, even though interest earnings are called "dividends."

5) Interest earned on proceeds of insurance left on deposit
with an insurance company. For example, if you are the beneficiary of your spouse's insurance policy and you elect to receive the
payments in installments based on a guaranteed rate—not in a
lump sum—then the interest earned on proceeds left with the
insurance company will be taxed.

Municipal Bonds: Tax-Exempt Interest Line 8b

Municipal bonds issued by states, cities, and local governments,
and by their agencies, are one of the few tax-exempt investments
available. Nevertheless, you must report the interest income on
Line 8b of Form 1040. It is not part of your taxable income, but it
may increase the amount of Social Security benefits that are
subject to taxation. In addition, some tax-exempt income is used
in computing the alternative minimum tax liability.

Tax-exempt bonds are not protected by the market discount rule. If you sell at a profit, this profit must be reported as a capital gain on Line 13. Only the interest is tax-exempt.

Caution: Check with your broker or accountant; interest on certain types of municipal bonds is now subject to taxation.

Dividend Income Line 9

The most common dividends are cash distributions to stockholders of a company. Dividends can also be issued in the form of property, stock rights (the right to buy more stock at a special price), services, or extra cash distributions known as additional dividends. Most dividends paid by corporations and mutual funds are disbursed quarterly, but occasionally there are irregular or year-end dividends.

If you receive over $400 of dividend income you must use Form 1040 or 1040A to file your tax return. Report the dividend income in Part III of Form 1040A, and on Line 9 if you use Form 1040.

 Expenses related to earning dividend income may be deductible, but only if you itemize. They fall into the "Miscellaneous Deductions" category, in which items are deductible only if they total 2% of your adjusted gross income (see also Chapter 10).

If you own shares in a money market fund, your "interest" is actually a dividend. However, some bank money market accounts pay interest, not dividends. Regardless of what it's called, you must pay tax on it.

Dividend Reinvestment

An increasing number of companies allow shareholders to reinvest their dividends into additional shares of the company through a "dividend reinvestment plan." If you opt for this arrangement, you will receive a statement every quarter indicating how many more shares or fractional shares your dividends have purchased. The amount reinvested represents taxable income. You will receive

Form 1099-DIV from the company, indicating the amount you must report as taxable income.

Capital Gains Distributions

If you own shares in a mutual fund or a REIT (real estate investment trust), you may receive capital gains distributions. These distributions are made when the fund or REIT sells its holdings or investments and receives a capital gain.

The Form 1099-DIV (or other annual statement) you receive from the fund will tell you what portion is a capital gains distribution. Report this amount on Lines 13 and 14 of your Form 1040.

Mutual Fund Expenses

Mutual funds incur management and administrative expenses that are treated as capital expenses. In addition to telling you what your dividend distribution is, the mutual fund must tell you what your share of the expenses is. The fund's expenses—or, rather, your share—is a miscellaneous expense and can be added to other miscellaneous expenses; if they all add up to at least 2% of your adjusted gross income, they can be deducted. Nevertheless, these two items—dividend distribution and your share of the fund's expenses—must be added together and then reported as a dividend, all of which is taxable.

 If you manage your own investment account, the expenses involved are considered miscellaneous expenses and are subject to the 2% floor for deduction purposes. You can add the expenses to any other miscellaneous deductions you have.

Stock Splits

Sometimes a company distributes additional shares as a supplement to, or in lieu of, cash dividends. A stock split generally takes place when the price of the stock has reached an historically high price. A split does not make you richer or poorer—you merely hold more pieces of paper that together represent an investment of the same value. For example, you own 100 shares of a stock with a current market price of $50 per share for a total investment value of $5,000. Management declares a 2-for-1 split, which means you will now own 2 shares for every 1 you already had. Your total investment value is still $5,000, but you now have 200 shares valued at $25 per share. (You do not pay tax on a stock split, then, because there is no dollar increase to tax.)

6 Retirement Income

There are literally hundreds of types of retirement plans, annuities, and insurance programs offered today, each with differing tax consequences. This chapter offers only the basics on these plans, but will give you a general understanding of the IRS regulations in these areas, as well as show you ways to handle income from these various plans and policies. You should also consult your personnel officer or your accountant about your situation, and about whether you should participate in any particular plan. For more detailed information, read IRS publication #575, "Pension and Annuity Income."

Social Security

The retirement plan that applies to nearly every American is Social Security. If you receive Social Security benefits, you will also receive Form SSA-1099 each year by February 1, indicating in Box 5 the total benefits you received for the previous tax year. Keep this form, but do not submit it with your tax return. The amount given in Box 5 may be subject to tax if your income is over a certain figure, known as the "base" amount. In that case, however, the maximum taxable amount is 50% of your benefits.

Here's how to calculate what you may owe in taxes if you are receiving Social Security:

1) Write down your modified adjusted gross income.*

2) Add to that amount 50% of your Social Security benefits.

3) If this total exceeds the base amount of $25,000 (filing as single), or $32,000 (filing jointly), or zero (for a married filing a separate return—unless he or she lived separately from the spouse for the full year, in which case they both are treated as singles), you will be taxed.

4) The amount of benefits on which you would owe tax is 50% of the excess over the base amount, or 50% of the total benefits, whichever is less.

For example:
• You and your spouse receive $10,000 in Social Security benefits, plus $12,000 from a fully taxable pension and $6,000 in taxable interest income. Your spouse also received $1,000 interest in tax-free municipal bonds.

• You file a joint return.

• Your adjusted gross income is $18,000 ($12,000 plus $6,000).

• Your modified adjusted gross income is $19,000 ($18,000 plus $1,000).

• Your modified adjusted gross income plus one-half of your Social Security benefits ($5,000) is $24,000, which does not exceed the base amount of $32,000; therefore, your Social Security benefits are not taxable.

Let's vary the example:
• You file a joint return.

• Your adjusted gross income is $18,000 ($12,000 in taxable pension plus $6,000 in taxable interest income).

• You also have $15,000 in tax-exempt municipal bond interest.

---

*Modified adjusted gross income is your adjusted gross income (*including* all foreign earned income and *excluding* Social Security benefits), plus your tax-exempt interest.

• Your modified adjusted gross income is therefore $33,000 ($18,000 + $15,000).

• You have $10,000 in Social Security benefits; $33,000 plus one-half of your Social Security benefits ($5,000) equals $38,000, which exceeds the base of $32,000 by $6,000. Since you have exceeded the base, you must pay tax. But how much?

• One-half of $6,000 is $3,000. This is the amount that is subject to tax because it is less than one-half of your Social Security benefits, which is $5,000.

Note: If you are married and file a separate return, the base amount is zero; therefore, one-half of your Social Security benefits is subject to tax no matter what the amount of your benefits or of your other income. But, if you lived apart from your spouse all year long and you file separately, the $25,000 base applies.

 You can reduce the Social Security benefits that are subject to tax by deferring other income. One way is to use Series EE savings bonds, which are not taxed until redeemed on maturity. Single-premium life insurance and deferred annuities (see page 44) also allow interest earned to be deferred from taxes until withdrawn, and unlike interest earned on municipal bonds, it is not added back into your income for the purpose of calculating your Social Security tax.

Qualified Company Retirement Plans   Line 17

A qualified plan is an employer-sponsored plan that meets various legal requirements. Qualified plans include pension, profit sharing, stock bonus, and employee stock ownership plans. Contributions and earnings on contributions that accumulate within the plan are usually not taxed to employees until the funds are distributed.

Rollovers and Distributions

If you receive or decide to take a distribution from an IRA or a qualified plan, you can "roll it over" into an IRA or another qualifying plan (of your new employer). The rollover must be made within 60 days after the receipt of the money, and cannot include non-deductible contributions to the plan.

Distributions from qualified plans fall into one of two categories, total or partial:

Total distribution: When one or more distribution takes place within one year, totaling all that is due the recipient from the account. Total distributions are treated more favorably than partial distributions.

Partial distribution: When at least 50% of the balance is distributed. The amount not rolled over in 60 days is taxed as ordinary income. A partial distribution can be made only because of disability, separation from service, or death.

Tax Treatment

The following points apply to qualified plans, IRA's, and tax-sheltered annuities:

1) If you receive your distribution in a lump sum (see box on page 43), you can reduce the amount of tax due on that portion your employer contributed by using the special 5-year averaging rule. With 5-year averaging, your distribution is not taxed all at once—instead, you are taxed as if you had received one-fifth of the distribution in each of the next 5 years, beginning with the first year you receive the money. This generally reduces your tax bill. You must fill out Form 4972 when averaging.

2) If you receive a lump-sum distribution in company securities, the appreciation on those securities is not taxed until you sell the stock.

3) If you take any money out before age 59½, you will be penalized 10% of the amount withdrawn, unless you are disabled. Nor would there be a penalty to your estate if the cash were distributed to your beneficiary, were you to die before age 59½. The penalty does not apply to a lump-sum distribution because you left your place of work or because the plan was terminated,

41

provided in either case the funds are rolled over into an IRA or another qualified pension plan.

Other exceptions to the 10% penalty, besides disability or death, are: a) any distribution that is a scheduled series of periodic payments made over the projected life expectancy of the participant (and a beneficiary, if desired); b) distributions made to employees aged 55 or over who have met the plan's early retirement provisions; and c) distributions for certain medical expenses.

(TS) Avoid the 10% penalty for early withdrawal. If you must withdraw money from your IRA or other retirement plan before you reach 59½, you can avoid the 10% penalty if you elect to take the distribution as part of a series of periodic payments to be made over your projected life expectancy or that of your beneficiary in the event of your death. But once you start to take periodic distributions, they must continue until you are 59½, or until 5 years after you start, whichever is later.

---

4) There is a 15% tax on "excessive" distributions, those which exceed certain limitations. The limitations are $750,000 for lump sums qualifying for averaging, and $150,000 for IRA's and all other types of distributions.

For example, if you receive $200,000 in an IRA distribution that is not a rollover from your own account or a death benefit from the account of someone who named you his or her beneficiary, the penalty will be 15% of $50,000 (the excess over $150,000), which is $7,500. (*Note:* The limitations may be adjusted for inflation.)

5) Inadequate distributions are subject to penalties. If you do not begin taking distributions soon enough after you turn 70½—you must begin no later than April 1 of the calendar year following the calendar year in which you reach age 70½, even if you have not retired—you will be penalized. The penalty is especially stiff—a tax equal to 50% of your dollar shortage—*i.e.,* 50% of the difference between what you should have received and what you did receive.

QUALIFICATIONS OF A LUMP-SUM DISTRIBUTION

A payment must meet all of these requirements to be considered a lump-sum distribution:

- The entire distribution must be made within one of the employee's tax years (this is usually a calendar year).
- The distribution must represent the total balance of the employee's credit in the plan. A distribution of only part of the account cannot be considered a lump-sum distribution.
- The employee must have been a participant in the plan for a minimum of 5 years before the year in which the distribution is made, unless payment is made to a beneficiary because the employee died.
- The distribution must be made because of one of these factors: death, disability, leaving the workplace (resignation, retirement, layoff, or termination), termination of plan, or because the employee reached age 59½.

Life Insurance   Line 22

Life insurance, in addition to providing financial protection in the event of death, can provide tax benefits now as well. Here are the three most popular types of life insurance and the tax implications of each.

Whole Life Insurance

Whole life insurance—which pays the face amount of the policy upon the death of the insured—can be a tax shelter in the following ways:

1) During the years that you are making premium payments, the cash value of your policy grows at compounded interest rates. This increase is not taxed.

2) When you die, the proceeds paid out from your life insurance policy to a beneficiary are generally tax-free to the

43

beneficiary. However, if the beneficiary is entitled to a lump-sum settlement but elects to receive installment payments instead, then a part of each payment is taxable. Your insurance company will provide the calculations for you.

Universal Life Insurance

Universal life insurance provides the policyholder with greater control over how his or her life insurance policy is handled. Unlike whole life, in which premiums and investment rates are usually preset, universal life offers flexibility—at the policyholder's discretion—in both of these areas. The tax-shelter benefits are virtually the same as those for whole life, however.

Single-Premium Life Insurance

In this type of policy you make a single, or onetime, premium payment—often $5,000, $10,000, or more. A portion of your premium goes for insurance, and part goes into an investment fund. The fund grows tax-free over the years. In most single-premium policies you can borrow up to 90% of the cash buildup and you do not have to pay it back. When you die, the loan is deducted from the amount due your beneficiary.

Annuities   Line 17

An annuity is a contract sold by a life insurance company; it guarantees a fixed or variable payment to the holder sometime in the future, usually upon retirement. Money in an annuity accumulates tax-free or tax-deferred—depending on the type of plan you have—until withdrawn, at which time you may pay some tax on the payouts. Your employer or insurance company will tell you precisely how much of your payouts are taxed and how much are tax-free. It varies from policy to policy.

IRA's and Keogh Plans   Line 16

Distributions from IRA's and Keogh plans are taxed similarly to distributions from qualified retirement plans. If your contributions were tax-deductible ones, those contributions are taxed as ordinary income when they are withdrawn.

With IRA's only, however, if you made any *non*deductible contributions, you will get tax-free that portion of your distribution that equals the portion of your IRA account represented by nondeductible contributions.

For example:
- In 1987 you contribute $2,000 which is deductible.
- In 1988, you contribute another $2,000, but this is *non*deductible.
- By 1989, your IRA is worth $5,000, $1,000 of which is earned income.
- At the end of 1989 you withdraw $500. How much of that will be tax-free? Because the nondeductible portion of your account ($2,000) represents 40% of your total account ($5,000), 40% of your withdrawal (or $200) will be tax-free. The balance ($300) will be taxed as ordinary income.

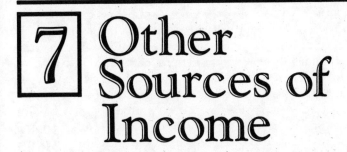

7 Other Sources of Income

Alimony

This is one of the most complex areas of the tax law, and while it is possible to address the basic rulings, if you are divorced, thinking about getting divorced, or even seeking a friendly, uncontested divorce—*be sure to seek professional advice.*

The rule of thumb is that alimony payments can be deducted by the one who pays them (the payor) and are taxable income for the one who receives them (the recipient).

This is exactly the opposite of the ruling on child-support payments: These and lump-sum property settlements are *not* deductible by the payor and are *not* taxable income for the recipient. What often happens, then, is that the partner who is paying tries to classify the bulk of the payments as alimony to make it tax deductible. Naturally, the recipient wants to maximize the amount that is considered child support, since that is not treated as taxable income.

If your divorce or separate maintenance agreement became effective on or after January 1, 1985, in order to qualify as alimony, a payment must usually be made under the terms of one of the following: 1) a decree of divorce or of separate maintenance; 2) a written instrument incident to divorce or separation; 3) a written separation agreement; or 4) a decree of support. It is imperative that one of these be in effect for payments to be accepted as alimony for tax purposes. Even if a verbal agreement between the parties labels payments as alimony, the IRS will not consider them alimony unless one of these conditions is met. (If your decree became effective before January 1, 1985, the rules are more complex and you should seek the advice of a professional.)

You may not use securities or property as alimony payments; they must be "cash." However, if the agreement specifies that the payments be made directly to a third party—say, for rent or medical expenses—they are usually allowed as alimony.

If you are involved in a divorce, you should also know that if you transfer to your spouse or ex-spouse property that has increased in value, he or she is not immediately taxed on the appreciation. The gain is taxed only upon the sale of the property. In other words, the burden of taxation is shifted from the payor to the recipient, but it kicks in only if the recipient elects to sell.

If you are receiving alimony, you will enter it on Line 11. If you are making alimony payments, you will enter the amount on Line 29.

Note: You do not need to itemize deductions in order to claim a deduction for alimony. Alimony payments are considered an adjustment to income for the payor. (See Chapter 8.)

You can avoid a $50 penalty when you fill out your return by making sure you provide the IRS with the name and Social Security number of the ex-spouse to whom you are paying alimony.

Barter

Line 12

When you trade your property or services for those of another, and no cash is exchanged, you have bartered. The IRS insists that you include the fair market value of any barter transaction as income. It is left up to you to assign the amount, and unless it's obviously lower than market value, it will be accepted.

For example, if you are an accountant and your friend is a dentist, and you provide accounting services in exchange for dental work, both of you must report the fair market value of the other's services as gross income on Schedule C, "Profit or Loss from Business or Profession."

 If you itemize, you may be able to claim the dental work you received in the barter example above as a medical expense. Check with your accountant.

If you belong to a bartering club, you will receive Form 1099-B, "Statement for Recipients of Proceeds from Real Estate, Broker, and Barter Exchange Transactions." Reconcile this amount with your own records. The IRS imposes penalties on those who do not report barter income.

Capital Gains

When an asset is sold for more than its original purchase price, the difference in value is labeled a capital gain. The most likely sources of capital gains are stocks, bonds, commodities, real estate, and payments you receive on installment sales.

All gains made from selling securities are taxed and must be reported as income. Your stockbroker will send you Form 1099-B, showing the securities you sold, which you will report on Schedule D. Even if you sell a stock at the end of 1988 and do not receive the money until 1989, you still must report the gain for 1988. In other words, gains must be reported for the year in which the sale takes place (the same holds true, by the way, for losses).

Real estate owners often receive capital gains when they sell their principal residence. If this applies to you, file Form 2119, "Statement Concerning Sale or Exchange of Personal Residence," and report any gain on Line 3 of Schedule D. Any capital gain that cannot be deferred must be reported on Schedule D—for example, the excess gain over the $125,000 that can be permanently excused if you were 55 or older when you sold your house. More details on real estate taxation are given in Chapter 13.

Damages

If you are injured and then receive damages as the result of a settlement or court award, the damages are *not* usually taxable. This is because the IRS regards damages as a replacement for loss, not as income. The ruling includes injuries or illnesses caused by someone else's actions or negligence (if you slip on an unshoveled, icy sidewalk, for example); if you are subject to medical malpractice or to a plane, train, car, or bus accident; or if you are harmed from exposure to toxic chemicals. It also encompasses libel, defamation, invasion of privacy, and mental anguish.

The exception to the rule is defamation directed at your business reputation, which causes a loss of income. This is considered an injury to business, and damages awarded are included in your gross income.

If you receive as damages reimbursement for medical expenses you deducted in a previous year, then the amount deducted and reimbursed is taxable. Or, if part of your damages are expressly designated for future medical expenses, you cannot deduct those medical expenses.

Note: The government has issued seemingly conflicting opinions where damages are concerned. Consult a professional if you have any questions.

Debts When Canceled · Line 22

In most cases, when a debt is "discharged" you must report it as gross income on Line 22, "Other income." A debt is considered discharged when it is forgiven, canceled, or settled for less than the full amount. The amount you must report is only the difference between the full debt and the amount you have actually paid off.

A similar rule applies to income from discharging debts through declaring bankruptcy, which entails a legal filing under Title 11 of the U.S. Tax Code. If you want more information on declaring bankruptcy, read IRS publication #908, "Bankruptcy," for a full understanding of the applicable rulings.

Sometimes student loans are reduced or totally forgiven if the student agrees to work for a public benefit corporation, for an agency of the government, or for certain educational organizations. For example, your $10,000 in student loans for medical school might be canceled if you work for a low-income-area hospital for several years after graduation.

Farm Income · Line 19

This is a highly specialized area; read IRS Publication #225, "Farmer's Tax Guide," to supplement the data given on Schedule F, which must be attached to your return.

Fees · Line 22

You must include in your taxable income fees received for these and other services:

- public speaking
- notary public services
- jury duty
- executor's or trustee's responsibilities
- referrals
- election precinct work

Foreign Income

Line 22

If you are a U.S. citizen or resident alien, you must file a U.S. tax return, even if all your money was earned abroad.

If you worked abroad you can exclude up to $70,000 of foreign earned income, plus housing allotments, *if* you meet all three of these requirements:

1) Your foreign income must be earned income;

2) Your "tax home" (*i.e.*, your principal place of business, not necessarily where your family is located) must be in a foreign country;

3) You must either be a resident of a foreign country for a full tax year, or be physically present in a foreign country or countries for 330 days during any consecutive 12-month period.

If you meet these requirements, you may also be able to exclude or deduct some of your housing costs. Check with an accountant and read IRS publication #54, "Tax Guide for U.S. Citizens and Resident Aliens Abroad." You will also need Form 2555, "Foreign Earned Income."

It is possible that you will have to pay foreign tax on your income earned abroad, but you can get tax breaks for it on your U.S. tax return. See page 75 for details.

Gambling Winnings

Line 22

Winnings at the roulette table—and elsewhere—are taxable income. Losses can be taken as itemized deductions, but only to the dollar amount of your winnings. For example, your winnings in Atlantic City for the year totaled $21,000, and your losses were $5,000. Your taxable income would be $16,000.

If you are a professional gambler, you may also subtract from your winnings any losses that do not exceed winnings, as well as reasonable expenses from the winnings income you must report on Schedule C.

If you get lucky and win the lottery or a raffle, your prize is considered taxable income—although you can deduct the price of the winning ticket. If you win property, such as a new car, you will be taxed on the fair market value of the property.

Gifts Line 22

A true gift is not taxable (although there are some limits; see point #8 on page 89 for an example). In the business world, however, the line is often blurred. If the reason for giving the gift is anticipated economic benefit for the giver, it may be taxable income to the recipient.

Illegal Payments Line 22

Believe it or not, extortion, ransom, embezzled money, bribes, and kickbacks are taxable income. If you find yourself in this unfortunate predicament, get a lawyer before doing anything else.

IRD Line 22

When someone dies, income to which that person was entitled but did not receive is called "income in respect of a decedent." It is taxable as income to the estate or beneficiary; if the estate or beneficiary is subject to federal estate tax, the estate or the beneficiary must pay this tax as well.

Moving Expenses

Moving expenses that are reimbursed by your employer are reportable as income on Line 7 of the Form 1040. This amount will be included in Box 10 on your form W-2 and you will receive Form

4782, showing the total amount paid, from your employer. You may, however, be able to take these moving-expense payments as an itemized deduction (see pages 66–67).

Prizes and Awards

Prizes and awards are generally taxable as income, and are reported on Line 22 of the Form 1040, although scholarships and fellowships for degree candidates are not taxable. If you've received an award after 1986 for achievement of a religious, scientific, literary, civic, or other similar nature, you may be able to avoid paying taxes on it if you transfer it to a qualified tax-exempt organization. Employee achievement awards are excluded from gross income only insofar as their cost is tax deductible to the employer.

Rents, Royalties, and Partnerships
Line 18

If you have any income in this category and it seems complicated to sort out, don't be surprised—it is (refer to Chapter 13 for the basics on rental income). You must report rental income on Line 18 of your Form 1040 and fill out Schedule E. Schedule E is also required for those who receive income from royalties, a partnership, an estate, or a trust.

Scholarships and Fellowships

If you are a degree candidate, scholarships and fellowships (up to the amount you spend for tuition, fees, books, supplies, and equipment required for your course work) are not taxed. Amounts received above these specific costs are taxed.

For example, you receive a $6,000 scholarship. The cost of

your tuition, fees, and housing is $4,500. You spend the rest on such items as movies, food, and clothes. That "rest" (*i.e.*, $1,500) is regarded as income.

Caution: If you are not a degree candidate, all payments made to you are considered part of your income.

 Student loans that are "forgiven" are usually exempt from taxation (see page 49).

Refunds of State and Local Income Taxes
Line 10

If you take as an itemized deduction the state or local taxes you pay, and then receive a refund of part of those taxes, you must report the refund as income for the year in which you receive it.

Welfare

In the unfortunate event that you or someone you know must collect welfare, it will probably come as a surprise to learn that the IRS will treat you with atypical kindness. Federal, state, and local benefits, including Aid to Families with Dependent Children, home relief, and emergency relief, are not taxed.

Other
Line 22

The IRS lumps miscellaneous tax-exempt payments in this category. These include awards paid by a crime victim's compensation board (except medical expenses previously deducted); payments to handicapped individuals employed under the Employment Opportunities for Handicapped Individuals Act; Medicare benefits; state benefits paid to the blind; and mortgage assistance payments under the National Housing Act and similar legislation.

8 Adjustments to Income

The Tax Code allows you to use certain expenses to reduce your taxable income—these are called deductions. In other words, you receive a small break for spending money on certain items.

You'll note that on Form 1040, the first category after "Income" is "Adjustments to Income." Don't be confused by the term *adjustments*. Adjustments are actually deductions, but extraspecial ones. On your tax form, they reduce your gross income right away; this is how you compute your "adjusted gross income." (True deductions, on the other hand, are subtracted later on. They are explained in Chapter 9.)

Adjustments are also referred to as "above-the-line" deductions because they are part of the calculations by which you arrive at the dollar amount on which *other* deductions—such as medical deductions—are based. One special advantage of adjustments is that they can also be claimed by those who do not itemize their deductions.

Remember, you always subtract adjustments from your income, but you can only subtract specific other deductions if you itemize. As explained in Chapter 9, itemizing is becoming more difficult because the "floors" are increasing, as is the standard deduction (a predetermined deductible amount for those who cannot itemize).

Adjustments to Income include six items. Each one is described below.

Reimbursed Employee Business Expenses Line 24

Many employees have job-related expenses, and for some—such as a salesperson—these expenses can be quite large. If you charge these expenses on your personal credit card, or pay for them in cash, you are, in effect, making a loan to your employer until you are reimbursed. You may adjust your gross income by the *total* amount of such reimbursed travel, entertainment, and transportation expenses. You must file Form 2106, "Employee Business Expenses," to do this. The amount you deduct cannot exceed the reimbursed amount.

For example, you incur $4,150 in business-related expenses, and are reimbursed for $3,000 of them. You may deduct the *entire* $3,000 from your gross income on Line 24. (Moreover, if you itemize your deductions, the unreimbursed $1,150 is deductible as a miscellaneous itemized deduction, provided your total miscellaneous itemized deductions meet the 2% floor. Only 80% of your unreimbursed meal and entertainment costs, however, may be applied toward the 2% floor.)

Your IRA Deduction Line 25

If you are not covered by a retirement plan at work, you do not have to pay taxes on up to $2,000 annually for your IRA (Individual Retirement Account) contribution. Even if you or your spouse is covered by a company pension plan, you can still make an adjustment for IRA deposits of up to $2,000—*if* your adjusted gross income is under $40,000 for those filing a joint return, or under $25,000 for those filing singly.

Complete the worksheet in the IRS instruction booklet in order to determine how much, if any, you can deduct for an IRA contribution if your income falls above these levels. Single taxpayers with adjusted gross incomes of $25,000 to $30,000 get a partial deduction if they have a pension plan at work; so do couples with joint incomes of $40,000 to $50,000. Even if you cannot make a deductible IRA contribution, you can still make a nondeductible contribution of up to $2,000 and take advantage of the tax-deferred buildup of cash inside an IRA.

Health Insurance for the Self-Employed
Line 26

If you are self-employed you can deduct up to 25% of the premium you pay for health insurance for yourself and your family. However, you cannot take this deduction if you qualify for coverage under another plan—for example, one provided by your spouse's employer. (See page 84 for more tax-savings hints for self-employed individuals with medical expenses.)

Keogh & SEP Deductions
Line 27

If you are self-employed you can make a tax-deductible contribution to a Keogh plan. In general, you can put in up to 20% of your gross self-employment income, and all of it is deductible.

A Simplified Employee Pension (SEP) plan is essentially an IRA, but the employer, not the employee, makes the contribution. SEP's were established to encourage employers to provide retirement benefits under a less complex arrangement than a qualified retirement plan. If you are self-employed or have a small proprietorship, you can easily open a SEP at your bank or brokerage firm by filling out the appropriate form.

In a SEP, contributions can be made of up to 13.04% of your self-employment income, or $30,000—whichever is less. Because you are self-employed, the entire contribution can be taken as an adjustment to your income since *you* are the employer.

Penalty on Early Withdrawal of Savings Line 28

Your bank will send you Form 1099-OID, showing any penalty charged because you took out money from a special time-savings account, such as a CD, before maturity. (These penalties do not apply to regular savings accounts.) You can adjust your income by the amount of penalty you pay.

Alimony Line 29

Alimony you pay, with the receiver's name and Social Security number listed, is entered on Line 29. (For more information on alimony, see Chapter 7.)

Total Adjustments Line 30

Total Lines 24 through 29 and enter the figure on Line 30. This constitutes your total adjustments.

Adjusted Gross Income Line 31

To arrive at your adjusted gross income, subtract your total adjustments (Line 30) from your gross income (Line 23). Enter this number on Line 31, and also on Line 32.

9 Itemized Deductions

Deductions are the expenses you can legitimately use to reduce your gross income or adjusted gross income. They lie at the heart of reducing your taxes.

The two types of deductions are the standard deduction and the itemized deductions. You can use only one—if you elect to itemize, for instance, then you cannot take the standard deduction, and vice versa. If you can document that you have incurred expenses for specific things such as medical and dental care, mortgage interest, real estate taxes, charitable contributions, or casualty losses, there is a good chance you will benefit from itemizing your deductions. Any itemized deductions you claim must be based on expenses you can actually substantiate, which means you must keep accurate records. If you cannot itemize, then you will take the standard deduction.

You will subtract your deductions—itemized or standard—from your adjusted gross income (which you entered on Lines 31 and 32). You will also use your adjusted gross income to figure your 7.5% floor for determining eligibility of medical deductions, and your 2% floor for eligibility of miscellaneous deductions.

Itemizing—Yes or No?

It pays to itemize only if all your itemized deductions add up to more than your standard deduction would be. Therefore, you must determine all your allowable deductions before deciding which system is better for you.

Among those for whom itemizing tends to be worthwhile are homeowners, residents of high-income-tax states, freelancers, and those with high medical deductions or charitable contributions.

If you itemize, you must attach *Schedule A* to your return. The major deductible items are listed below, but bear in mind that there are others; you may want to ask your accountant about something you think might be deductible.

Note: If you are married and filing separately, you should itemize if your spouse does. If your spouse itemizes and you do not, your standard deduction is set at $0.

Medical and Dental Expenses
Schedule A, Lines 1–4

You can deduct medical and dental expenses you incurred for yourself, your spouse, and your dependents, but first you must subtract the dollar amount of any insurance or other reimbursements you received. And, only those *unreimbursed* medical expenses that add up to more than 7.5% of your adjusted gross income can be deducted.

The definition of *dependent* has a special meaning when applied to medical expenses: It is any dependent for whom you claimed an exemption, but *also* includes anyone you *could* have claimed as a dependent but did not because his or her gross income was $1,950 or more or because he or she filed a joint return. It also includes an ordinarily non-dependent child of a divorced parent if the parent incurred medical expenses for that child.

Caution: You cannot deduct expenses made in connection with your general well-being—only those made to make you well if you are sick, or to preserve your health if you have a chronic ailment.

 If you are a divorced parent and pay for medical or dental care for your child, you are entitled to the deduction (providing you meet your 7.5% floor) *even if* the child is not your dependent and you do not take an exemption for him or her.

Acceptable Medical Deductions

These unreimbursed costs are deductible:

- Schooling of the handicapped, including cost of meals, lodging, and classes

- Hospital costs

- Doctors' and dentists' fees, including those of midwives, Christian Science practitioners, acupuncturists, and some homeopathic doctors

- Medical equipment

- Medical insurance premiums

- Prescription drugs

- Laboratory exams and tests

- Transportation to and from the doctor or dentist's office or other place of treatment

- Private-duty nurse's wages

- Drug-abuse clinics and alcoholism clinics

It may surprise you to learn that the following are also considered acceptable medical deductions:

- Costs of specially prepared foods (salt-free meals, for example) if advised by a doctor, even if purchased in a restaurant

- A home-care nurse, if medically required; this can include the nurse's fees, meals, and out-of-pocket expenses related to lodging

- Installation or rental of a fluoride machine in your home, if prescribed by a dentist

- False teeth; hearing aids; the cost of feeding and caring for a seeing-eye dog

- Cost of a special school for the mentally retarded, psychologically disturbed, or severely learning-disabled

- Birth-control methods, including vasectomies and tubal ligation

- Nursing and retirement home costs, if illness or need for medical care is the reason for being there

- Home improvements, if prescribed—for example, an elevator, an exercise pool, air conditioning (such as to relieve an allergy), or removal of lead paint if someone incurred lead poisoning

- Some voluntary surgery (but only if performed by a licensed professional), such as abortions, cosmetic surgery, hair transplants, and face-lifts

Unacceptable Medical Deductions

These costs are not accepted by the IRS as valid medical expenses for the purpose of deductions:

- Dancing lessons prescribed by a doctor as physical or mental therapy

- Ear piercing

- Deprogramming a cult member

- Health club dues

- Maternity clothes

- Health foods

- Nonprescription drugs, vitamins, toiletries

- Stop-smoking programs

- Most weight-reduction programs

- Funerals, cremations, burials, cemetery plots

- Hotel rooms for sex therapy

- Nurses for healthy babies

- Tattooing

- Vaccinations

Taxes You Paid Schedule A, Lines 5–8

Although sales taxes are no longer deductible, state and local income taxes, real estate taxes, and personal property taxes are, even if they are estimated payments. The total is entered on Line 8 of Schedule A. All real estate taxes are deductible. If your property taxes are included in your mortgage payment, which is often the case, you will receive a form from your lender each year showing the dollar amount for property taxes. If you sell property during the year, the taxes are prorated between you and the buyer. If you own a cooperative residence you can deduct a percentage of the cooperative corporation's taxes. The co-op will notify you of the amount.

Note: If you own a condominium, your real estate taxes are the same as those paid by "regular" homeowners.

Mortgage Interest Schedule A, Line 9

All interest on mortgage payments is deductible for your primary residence and one other home that you use at least 14 days a year. However, interest payments on a home you rent out as a business are not reported here; that's taken care of on Schedule E. List any deductible points on Line 10. (A point is equal to 1% of the total amount of the loan. Points are charged by a lender at the time of borrowing; see page 79 for details on points.)

Mortgage interest on a loan taken to upgrade your property or to finance medical educational expenses is also deductible, but *only* if the actual loan does not exceed the lesser of the fair market value of your home, or your adjusted basis. (Adjusted basis is the purchase cost of your home plus the cost of improvements.) Mortgage interest rules are complex; see Chapter 13 for more information.

Investment Interest Schedule A, Line 11

Interest on a loan used to buy or carry an investment—something that produces interest, dividends, or royalties, such as stocks and bonds—is deductible up to the amount of your net investment income. (To determine net investment income, take your investment income for the year—interest, dividends, annuities, royalties, and gains from sales of stocks and bonds—and subtract your deductible investment expenses.) Deductible investment interest is most likely to be found in a margin account, which is a brokerage account in which you can borrow from your broker to buy securities; your broker charges you interest for this loan. Deductible investment expenses are discussed in Chapter 17.

 If your investment interest is greater than your net investment income, you can deduct 40% of the excess interest, up to $4,000, in 1988; 20%, up to $2,000, in 1989; 10%, up to $1,000, in 1990; but none thereafter.

Personal Loan
Interest Schedule A, Line 12a

Deduction of interest on credit cards (such as Visa, MasterCard, or other charge cards), personal and student loans, car loans, and other types of consumer loans is being phased out. By 1991 there will be no deductions for this type of interest. In the meantime, 40% is deductible for 1988; for 1989, 20%; and 10% for 1990. The total amount of interest paid is entered on Line 12a of Schedule A.

Charitable
Contributions Schedule A, Lines 14–17

Giving to your church, your alma mater, or a bona fide charity is tax deductible. Contributions you made by check are reported on Line 14 of Schedule A. Be ready to provide details for contributions over $3,000. If you claim more than $500 worth of clothing, artwork, furniture, or other gifts that are not cash, you must fill out Form 8283 and enter the amount on Line 15.

If you give property worth $5,000 or more, it is wise to have it appraised and have the charity sign the appraiser's document. The IRS is zealous in checking this kind of contribution.

Before giving to any charity, make absolutely certain it is one qualified by the IRS. If you have any doubts, check with the organization, or, better still, directly with the IRS. Many charitable organizations that have received approval are listed in IRS publication #78, the so-called "Blue Book of Charities."

Note: If you charge your contribution on your charge card, it is deductible at the time of the charge, not when you pay your bill.

NONDEDUCTIBLE DONATIONS

Gifts to the following organizations are not deductible:
- Social clubs
- Business organizations
- Most foreign organizations
- Communist organizations
- Chambers of commerce
- Political parties or candidates
  Also, you cannot deduct:
- Blood donations
- Gifts of rent-free property
- Amount paid to use a religious hall
- Loan to a charity
- Price of raffle tickets
- Parochial school tuition

There is another valid charity-related deduction that many people overlook—unreimbursed expenses incurred when you do volunteer work for a charity. This includes the cost of uniforms, postage, stationery, equipment, advertising, and other expenses. If you drive in connection with your charitable activities, you may deduct 12 cents per mile for gas, as well as tolls and parking fees—but not maintenance, depreciation, or insurance on your car. If you take public transportation, the actual cost is deductible.

Keeping Good Records

In order to validate your contribution, you must keep either: 1) a canceled check; or 2) a receipt or letter from the organization showing the name of the organization, the date, and the amount donated. For small cash contributions, if you have none of the above, the IRS will usually accept your word.

A worksheet for recording your charitable contributions appears in the Appendix of this book.

(TS) If you buy benefit performance tickets that include an additional contribution over and above the regular cost of the tickets, the tickets are deductible—but only to the extent of the difference between the regular admission and the cost of the benefit ticket. However, if you return the tickets to the charity for it to resell because you cannot attend, then the entire dollar amount you paid is deductible.

Casualty and Theft Losses
Schedule A, Line 18

Losses that are the result of casualty or theft of your personal property are partly deductible. There are two limitations: 1) You must subtract $100 for each casualty loss (determining the value of the loss can be a complicated procedure; your insurance company will give you guidance); 2) Total yearly losses are deductible only to the extent that the total loss amount exceeds 10% of your adjusted gross income.

You must be able to prove: 1) you owned the property; 2) the amount of the loss; and 3) that the loss was sudden, in the case of a casualty. (A casualty loss is one that is sudden, unexpected, or unusual; most are caused by external or natural forces and are listed in the box below.)

Always report your loss to the police and get a copy of their report or file number to substantiate your claim to the IRS. *And,* have your belongings photographed or videotaped now, especially your valuables. Do not keep the pictures, videotape, receipts, or appraisals in your home, where they, too, could be stolen or destroyed—they are safest in a safety-deposit box.

CASUALTY LOSSES

Damage caused by the following is deductible:
- Storms
- Floods
- Fires
- Earthslides
- Sudden sinking of land
- Hurricanes
- Windstorms
- Earthquakes
- Automobile accidents
- Thefts during blackouts

Damage caused by the following is *not* deductible:
- Erosion of coastline
- Animals
- Termites or other insects
- Birds

Moving Expenses   Schedule A, Line 19

Moving expenses you incur are deductible *only* if you itemize your deductions. (If your employer reimburses you for, or even directly pays for, your moving expenses, the amount must be reported as income on your tax return, and then may be eligible as a deduction.) You can deduct moving expenses only if the move is business-related and if your expenses meet numerous IRS requirements. For details, consult IRS publication #521, "Moving Expenses." The deduction is designed to compensate you to some degree for a job-related expense. Moving expenses are not subject to the 2% floor, and if you take the deduction, it must be either as a business expense or as a moving expense; it cannot be both. If you itemize moving expenses, you must also attach Form 3903 or 3903F.

DEDUCTIBLE MOVING EXPENSES

The following moving expenses are considered acceptable deductions:

• Packing, crating, and transportation costs of moving furniture and household belongings;

• Temporary storage for up to 30 consecutive days;

• Insurance costs;

• Meals, lodging, and transportation costs for you and your family incurred en route to your new home (meals, however, are subject to the 80% limitation, which means costs must be reduced by 20% before you can deduct them as part of your moving expenses);

• Travel expenses to look for a new home *after* getting a job—*i.e.*, pre-move house-hunting trips;

• Meals and lodging for up to 30 consecutive days while in temporary quarters after getting a new job and leaving your old home;

• Expense of selling your old home and buying or renting a new one, including real estate agent's commissions, attorney's fees, and escrow fees;

• Cost of moving a pet;

• Cost of shipping an automobile;

• Cost of connecting and disconnecting utilities when moving appliances (connecting a telephone in your new home is *not* deductible).

Note: The deductions for house-hunting trips and temporary lodging combined cannot be more than $1,500. The total cost of these two items plus expenses for selling and buying or renting a new home cannot exceed $3,000.

Miscellaneous Deductions

Schedule A, Lines 20–24

The IRS allows you to take certain miscellaneous itemized deductions provided their total exceeds 2% of your adjusted gross income. On Line 20, enter unreimbursed employee business expenses and attach Form 2106. (Employee expenses can include travel, meals, and entertainment; see Chapters 8 and 15.) On Line 21 enter other expenses (see box, below).

ALLOWABLE MISCELLANEOUS DEDUCTIONS (SUBJECT TO 2% FLOOR)

The IRS will let you deduct the following miscellaneous expenses, provided these plus any unreimbursed business expenses meet the 2% floor:

- Tax preparation fees;
- The cost of this book and other tax preparation manuals;
- Tax attorney and accountant fees incurred in connection with income-producing property, or a business or employment issue (but legal expenses for personal matters are not usually deductible);
- The cost of investment advice;
- The cost of investment publications;
- Unreimbursed employee expenses;
- Union dues;
- IRA and Keogh plan custodial fees;
- Job-hunting expenses, only if in your same field of work;
- The cost of work uniforms and cleaning them;
- Safety-deposit box rental fees, if the box is used to store income-producing securities;
- Hobby expenses, up to the dollar amount earned from the hobby;
- Education expenses, to maintain your present salary or job;
- Fees paid to collect interest or dividends.

Other Miscellaneous Deductions

Schedule A, Line 25

Some miscellaneous deductions that are *not* subject to the 2% floor and may be deducted *in full* are: 1) gambling losses, up to the extent of winnings; 2) occupational expenses incurred by a handicapped worker, such as the cost of special tools; 3) estate taxes, in rare and unusual cases. These are entered on Line 25 of Schedule A. For more information on these and other expenses not subject to the 2% floor, see IRS publication #529, "Miscellaneous Deductions."

The total amount of all your itemized deductions is entered on Line 26 of Schedule A *and* on Form 1040, Line 34.

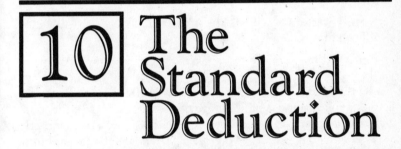

10 The Standard Deduction

The next section of Form 1040, labeled "Tax Computation," covers your deductions plus several additional steps necessary to determine your final tax bill.

On Line 32 you will enter your adjusted gross income, and on Line 34 the larger of either your standard deduction or your itemized deductions. Itemized deductions were discussed in the previous chapter. Let's look at the standard deduction to see if it's right for you. (Of course, if your itemized deductions exceed your standard deduction, you should itemize.)

The Standard Deduction Line 34

Taxpayers who cannot itemize because they do not have expenses for things like medical costs or mortgage interest are entitled to a standard deduction. The dollar amount of this deduction is determined by the IRS. The amount of the standard deduction varies according to your filing status and age.

THE STANDARD DEDUCTION

Filing Status	Amount for 1988
Single	$3,000
Married filing jointly	5,000
Married filing separately	2,500
Head of household	4,400
Qualifying widow(er)	5,000

Note: Starting in 1989, the standard deduction will be adjusted for inflation.

Additional Standard Deduction Line 33a

If you or your spouse is blind or age 65 or older, you are entitled to a greater standard deduction (see box below). Check the appropriate boxes on your tax return on Line 33a. The IRS defines as blind a person who cannot see better than 20/200 in his or her stronger eye with glasses, or whose field of vision is not more than 20 degrees. A taxpayer who is over 65 *and* also blind is entitled to two increased deductions, one for each situation.

ADDITIONAL STANDARD DEDUCTION

Filing Status	$ Increase	
	Over 65	**Blind**
Single	$750	$750
Married filing jointly	600	600
Married filing separately	600	600
Head of household	750	750
Qualifying widow(er)	600	600

To determine your total standard deduction, take the basic standard deduction and add it to the additional deduction, if one applies. For example:

Basic deduction, married filing jointly	$5,000
You are age 66	600
Your spouse is 69	600
You are blind	600
	$6,800

Tax Computation Lines 32–40

Subtract Line 34 from Line 32 and enter the figure on Line 35. Then multiply $1,950 by the total number of exemptions you claimed on Line 6e and enter that figure on Line 36. To obtain your taxable income, subtract Line 36 from Line 35 and enter it on Line 37.

Note: If you are computing taxes for a dependent child under age 14 who has over $1,000 of unearned income (interest, dividends, etc.), you should probably have their taxes figured out on Form 8615, "Computation of Tax for Children Under Age 14 Who Have Investment Income of More Than $1,000." The excess over $1,000 is taxed at the parent's rate, not the child's. See also page 88 for further information on when a child must file a return.)

11 Tax Credits

In the next section of your Form 1040, you have an opportunity to further reduce your taxes by taking certain credits. Credits are more valuable than deductions because they are dollar-for-dollar reductions of your actual tax, whereas deductions only reduce your taxable income. In other words, a dollar of credit is worth a dollar of taxes saved. That's why it pays to get all the credits you can. Here are the major tax credits and how you can make the most of them:

Child- and Dependent-Care Credit

Line 41

If you pay child- or dependent-care expenses so you and your spouse can work—or so that one of you can work and the other can go to school—you may be able to take a tax credit of up to 30% of these expenses. You must attach Form 2441, which explains exactly how to calculate the amount of credit you can take. The maximum credit can be up to $720 if there is one qualifying person in your home or $1,440 if there is more than one.

To claim the credit you must meet all four of the following requirements:

1) The payments must allow you to work or look for work. (If you work and your spouse is in school, you can still claim the credit.)

2) You must earn income during the year. If you are a full-time student or disabled, you are considered to have $200 of earned income for every month, or $400 per month if there are two qualifying persons in your home.

3) You must pay over half the cost of keeping up your principal home.

4) If you were married at the end of the calendar year, you must file a joint return, *unless* you are legally separated or you were living apart from your spouse for the last 6 months. In that case, the qualifying dependent must have lived with you for over 6 months and you must have provided over half the costs of keeping up your home.

Qualifying Persons

A qualifying person is any one of the following:
- A dependent child under the age of 15;
- A mentally or physically handicapped person whom you could claim as a dependent or could have claimed except that he or she had gross income of $1,950 or more;
- Your spouse, who is mentally or physically unable to care for himself or herself.

Work-related expenses include those paid for:
- A housekeeper, maid, or cook, including their meals and lodging;
- A day-care center or nursery school;
- A babysitter;
- Summer day camp (not sleep-away camp);
- Room and board at boarding school (but not tuition).

Tuition costs are not allowable for children in the first grade and above, nor is transportation to and from school. A number of other special situations and rulings pertaining to this credit are discussed in IRS publication #503, "Child and Dependent-Care Credit and Employment Taxes for Household Employees."

How to Calculate the Credit

Qualified expenses can be as much as $2,400 if you have one qualifying person, or up to $4,800 if you care for two or more. The amount of the credit varies depending upon your income. If your adjusted gross income is $10,000 or less, your credit is 30% of these expenses if there is one qualifying person; if there are two or more, your credit is 30% of up to $4,800 of expenses. If your adjusted gross income is over $10,000, for every extra $2,000 you have the percentage rate decreases by 1%. Therefore, if your adjusted gross income is over $28,000, you can claim a maximum of 20% or $480 for one, and $960 for two or more dependents.

Credit for the Elderly or Disabled Line 42

If you are 65 or older, or even if you are under 65 but have retired due to permanent disability and receive taxable disability income, you may be able to get a tax credit of up to $1,125. However, your adjusted gross income must be $17,500 or less if you are single, and $20,000 for married couples. There are other complicated income qualifications, which are spelled out on Schedule R. You must attach Schedule R to your return in order to claim the credit.

Caution: You cannot claim this credit if you file Form 1040A or Form 1040EZ.

Earned Income Credit Line 56

Although the earned income credit is actually reported on Line 56, it is included here because it falls under the category of tax credit.

This credit is designed for low-income workers with families. To be eligible, you must meet the following qualifications:

1) Your 1988 adjusted gross income must be under $17,000.

2) You must maintain a household for yourself and your child.

3) The child must earn less than the dependency exemption ($1,950 in 1988), unless the child is under 19 or a full-time student.

4) If you are married you must file a joint return.

To determine if you qualify, complete the worksheet contained in the instructions that accompany Form 1040 or 1040A. The maximum credit for 1987 was $851. This figure is adjusted annually for inflation.

 If your earned income credit is greater than your total tax liability, the IRS will refund the extra amount.

Foreign Tax Credit Line 43

If you work outside the U.S. you may claim the foreign income taxes you pay either as a credit or as an itemized deduction. If you elect the credit, attach Form 1116. Generally you receive a larger tax reduction with a credit than with a deduction, although you may want to compute it both ways.

It is advisable to read IRS publication #514, "Foreign Tax Credit for U.S. Citizens and Resident Aliens," if this situation applies to you.

General Business Credit Line 44

The IRS groups several credits under this heading: the housing rehabilitation credit, targeted job credit, research credit, and low-income housing credit. These credits generally apply to higher-income taxpayers or businesses and therefore are not discussed in this book.

12 Other Taxes and Payments

Other Taxes Lines 48–53

After granting various tax credits, the IRS resumes its role as tax collector in the next section of Form 1040. Lines 48–61 cover a wide variety of special taxes, some of which may apply to you.

Self-Employment Tax   Line 48

If you make more than $400 from self-employment you are subject
to this tax, even if you do part-time work, freelance, or work as an
independent contractor. The tax is 13.02% of your first $45,000 of
net self-employment income. The tax is computed on Schedule
SE, "Computation of Social Security Self-Employment Tax."

 If you have several businesses from which you obtain
self-employment income, combine the net income so
that any losses you might have can be used to offset
income in one of the other businesses. This will reduce
your taxes.

Alternative Minimum Tax   Line 49

This tax is designed to make certain that high-income taxpayers
do indeed pay taxes. It does not apply to single taxpayers with
yearly incomes of $30,000 or less, to married taxpayers filing
jointly with yearly incomes of $40,000 or less, or to married
taxpayers filing separately with yearly incomes of $20,000 or less.

Tax from Recapture Investment
Credit   Line 50

Line 50 refers to credits claimed in previous years on certain
business equipment. These credits were repealed in 1986 and
normally apply to those earning above-average incomes.

Social Security Tax on Tip Income
Not Reported To Employer   Line 51

If you receive over $20 of tips in a month working for one employer
and you do not report it to the employer, you still must pay tax on
it, using Form 4137. If you do not, there is a penalty of 50% of the
Social Security tax due, in addition to the tax due.

Tax on IRA's
or Qualified Retirement Plans   Line 52

You may owe this tax if you received an early distribution or excess distributions from your retirement plan, or if you made excess contributions to these plans. Use Form 5329, "Return from Individual Retirement Savings" to see if you must pay such a tax.

Payments   Lines 54–65

On the next section of Form 1040, record the tax payments you have already made. Enter each payment on its appropriate line, then follow the steps in Lines 61–65 to determine whether you must pay more tax or are entitled to a refund.

After including your Social Security number, signature, occupation, and other necessary signatures from your spouse and/or tax preparer, you have completed your return!

PART TWO

Tailor-Made Tax Breaks

13 If You Own Real Estate

Although the 1986 Tax Reform Act cut back on some of the more generous and even outlandish tax breaks, a great many advantages still remain for those who own real estate and understand the laws. Here are fourteen of the best tax-saving tips for property owners.

1) Be sure to deduct all the mortgage interest and property taxes you pay on both your primary residence and one other home that you use at least 14 days a year (see also tip #8).

2) Interest charges on consumer loans to buy a recreational vehicle ("RV") and/or a boat are considered mortgage interest rather than interest on a personal loan, if the vehicle passes the second-residence test. To meet these requirements, the boat or RV must have a kitchen, toilet, and sleeping facilities. The advantage: Interest on a mortgage is fully deductible, whereas the deduction for interest on consumer loans is being phased out and will be nonexistent in 1990.

3) Deduct late-payment charges on your mortgage.

Banks do not always include these charges on their year-end statements, so refer to your own records and canceled checks for details.

4) Deduct mortgage points. These interest charges, sometimes required to get a mortgage loan, can be deducted if you are getting a new mortgage. They are also deductible if you are refinancing, provided they are prorated over the life of the mortgage. Points are paid when the mortgage is granted, and you must pay for your points with a separate check (*i.e.*, do not lump them in with a regular mortgage payment) in order to qualify for the deduction.

5) You may be exempt from tax on up to $125,000 of profit. If you are 55 or older, you can take the once-in-a-lifetime exemption from taxes on up to $125,000 of gains made from the sale of your home. You must be 55 before the date of sale and must have owned and occupied the house as your principal residence for 3 out of the last 5 years.

Caution: Neither you nor your spouse can have used this onetime exclusion before. Even a newly married couple who owns property jointly can get the exclusion *only* if neither has taken it before. Two homeowners over 55 who plan to marry, therefore, should sell prior to the ceremony in order for *each* to get a break on up to $125,000 of gains on the sale of their respective homes (provided neither has taken this break before). Joint owners over 55 who are *not* married, however, are each entitled to an exemption of up to $125,000 of his or her share of the profit on the sale of a home they own together (provided, again, they have not taken this break before).

6) If you are under 55 and you want to move, but do not want to forgo the tax break for sellers over 55, you can rent your home for up to 2 years prior to selling and then claim the $125,000 exemption. Remember, you must be 55 when you sell the property.

7) Defer taxes on your profits. You can defer taxes due when you sell your home—no matter what your age—if you buy a new primary residence of equal or greater value. The new residence must be purchased and occupied within two years of the sale of the first home.

8) Take vacation-home tax breaks. You can deduct mortgage interest and property taxes on your vacation house as long as *you* use it at least 14 days a year or 10% of the amount of time it's

79

rented—whichever is more. Although you must report rental income, you can also write off your rental expenses—utilities, insurance, repairs, maintenance, and depreciation—up to the amount of rental income you receive.

9) Don't report rental income if you rent out your vacation home for 14 days or less per year. Of course, you cannot deduct expenses, either, in this situation, but you can still deduct real estate taxes, casualty losses, and mortgage interest on loans up to the value of the second home, plus any improvements. If your mortgage was in place before August 16, 1986, full mortgage interest can be deducted against ordinary income.

10) Deduct up to $25,000 for property management. If you file as a single or as a married couple filing jointly, if your adjusted gross income is $100,000 or less, and if you actively manage a piece of rental property of which you own at least 10%, you can deduct up to $25,000 in expenses (including interest and depreciation), in excess of rental income, against "other" income. (For married couples filing separately, each person is entitled to deduct $12,500 in expenses, provided his or her income is $50,000 or less and the couple did not live together at all during the year. Married couples who did live together are not entitled to these deductions if they file separately.) Other income includes wages, salary, dividends, and interest income. Qualifying as an "active" manager is not difficult. You must approve tenants, decide on rental terms, authorize repairs, and own at least 10% of the property. As with all real estate activities, keep accurate, up-to-date records to document your "active" role.

11) Decide between improvements and repairs. Keep in mind that the cost of *improvements* cannot be deducted immediately; they can only be depreciated: over 27.5 years for residential and over 31.5 years for commercial real estate, purchased after 1986; if purchased before that, use the depreciation method that was established in past returns. On the other hand, the cost of *repairs* can be deducted in the year they are made, which offers an immediate tax advantage. To boost your tax deductions, therefore, emphasize repairs over improvements—for example, repair a leaky roof rather than put on a new one.

12) Deduct every allowable expense associated with rental property. This includes depreciations, fire insurance, cost of advertising for tenants, cleaning, travel expenses, legal fees, architectural fees, accounting fees, supplies, water, fuel taxes, repainting, rewallpapering, fixing leaks, calling in the exterminator. Remember, to meet the IRS definition of rental property, *your* personal use of the house must be limited to 10% of the number of days it is rented out, or 14 days, per year—whichever is *greater*.

13) Eliminate consumer debt. Turn your consumer debt into a fully deductible equity loan. Annual interest on consumer loans—for cars, boats, personal loans, and on credit cards—is extremely high, often topping 19%. An alternative: Borrow up to $100,000 (on top of your existing mortgage) through a home equity loan and use the money to pay off your consumer loans. Not only will the interest rate be lower, but the interest is still *fully* deductible. (The deductibility of interest on consumer loans, on the other hand, is being phased out; only 20% will be deductible in 1989.)

You can borrow up to $100,000 regardless of what your home originally cost, provided the new total debt on your home is not greater than its current market value.

Caution: Don't take out a home equity loan without a great deal of thought; $100,000 is a lot of money. Keep in mind, too, that closing costs will boost the actual cost of the loan. But if you do decide on a home equity loan, and you get an adjustable-rate one, remember that it works well when rates go down, but is expensive when rates go up—so look for a loan that carries a lid on future interest rate increases.

14) You need not pay very much tax on a home "exchange." If you exchange houses and the trade is an even one, you will not be taxed on that exchange. If you receive cash in addition, you will be taxed on the dollar gain only. For example, your old house is worth $60,000 and you exchange it for another one worth $63,000. You also get $1,000 in cash. Your value gain is $4,000, but your taxable gain is only $1,000.

14 | If You Work At Home

For many Americans, their workplace is at home, either full- or part-time. These taxpayers free-lance, own their own business, or, with the consent of their employer, do some of their work at home as well as at an office. The benefits are many: There are fewer or no commuting costs, a small work wardrobe is all that's needed, and at-home lunches and snacks are cheaper. And there are also some key tax-savers of which they can take advantage. Read each of the deduction tips below to see if any apply to your work situation.

(**Note:** If you operate a business or practice a profession as a sole proprietorship, fill out Schedule C, "Profit or Loss from a Business or Profession.")

What You Can Deduct

1) The cost of a home office. To qualify, part of your home must be set aside and used "regularly and exclusively" for business. It must be either your principal place of business or where you meet with clients, patients, or customers to conduct business. It must be "separately identifiable" if it's part of your house; it can also be a separate structure from your main house. If you are an employee and you do some of your work at home, your home office must be used in connection with your work and the arrangement must suit your employer.

Your deductions cannot be more than the net income produced by using your home office. Your net income is your income

82

minus expenses related to the business, such as supplies and wages. You cannot deduct items that only benefit your personal living space, but you can deduct the allocatable share of real estate taxes, heat, water, electricity, repairs, maintenance, air conditioning, and depreciation.

2) Often-overlooked home-office expenses. Proportionate costs of the following are also deductible: air-conditioner and heating repairs, a cleaning person, driveway repairs, and exterior painting—but not lawn care.

3) Excess home-office deductions. The Tax Reform Act of 1986 limits the amount of certain expenses you may take as deductions, based on your business income. However, qualified expenses you incurred but were unable to use can be carried over from one year to the next.

4) Your computer. The IRS says you can write off up to $10,000 of the total cost of your computer the year you buy it, if it is used exclusively for business at your regular business office, which can be your home office if it qualifies. In some cases this deduction also extends to using your computer to manage your own investments, but your computer must be used at least 50% of the time for business or investment purposes. Or, you can depreciate the full cost of your computer over several years. (You *must* depreciate its value if you do not meet the 50% requirement.) Note that the $10,000 write-off can be taken against income only, not against losses. If you spend more than $10,000, you may carry forward the excess until it has been written off in full.

5) Business casualty losses. If you were not reimbursed by your insurance company, these losses are fully deductible, whereas with personal casualty losses there is a $100 deduction per claim. If you suffer a business casualty, consult your insurance agent immediately.

6) Keogh or SEP plans. You can reduce your taxable income with a Keogh or SEP plan if you are self-employed (see page 56).

7) Fun. If you give a picnic, holiday party, or other traditional get-together for your employees, it is fully tax deductible (in other cases, only 80% of the cost of business meals and entertainment is deductible). The event, however, must be open to *all* employees if it is to be considered fully deductible. (See IRS publication #463, "Travel, Entertainment, and Gift Expenses," for more suggestions on possible deductions.)

8) Travel and entertainment. If you are a self-employed taxpayer, you can deduct travel and other costs from your business earnings on Schedule C. Although you may deduct only 80% of the cost of business-related meals and entertainment, you are not subject to the 2% floor that applies in the case of unreimbursed business expenses incurred by a person who is not self-employed. Keep good records and document the fact that a business discussion took place before, during, or after the event.

9) A break for performing artists. If you are a performing artist and your adjusted gross income is $16,000 or less, you can also take your deductions on Schedule C, where they are not subject to the 2% floor. To qualify as a performing artist, you must perform for at least two employers during the year, have total business deductions that exceed 10% of the income received for performing, and have an adjusted gross income of $16,000 or less.

10) Health insurance premiums. As a self-employed person, you can deduct as a business expense 25% of health insurance premiums paid to cover yourself and your family, provided you are not eligible for coverage under any other plan. The remaining 75% of the premiums you paid can be included with the other medical care expenses you deduct on Schedule A—subject, of course, to the 7.5% floor on those medical expenses.

11) Social Security Tax Overpayments. The maximum wage subject to Social Security tax is $45,000. Although overpayment is fairly rare, if you work for two employers it may happen.

12) Your hobby, if it is also a business. If you earn money from your hobby, you can claim deductions for related expenses, up to the amount of income gained from the hobby. But to deduct losses as well as expenses, you must show a profit for 3 of the last 5 years, unless you raise and race horses. With horses you need to show a profit for only 2 out of 7 years.

To prove to the IRS that your hobby is indeed a business, your records must be thorough. Keep a set of books, and set up a separate checking account. For example, a full-time schoolteacher who also works part-time as a photographer, taking wedding and other party pictures, can write off the cost of attending a photographer's convention if he or she can prove to the IRS that he or she is in the photography business—even if only part of the time.

13) You can deduct the cost of special clothes for work—if they are required for your job. You can also deduct the cost of cleaning them. Among those clothing items accepted as deductible by the IRS are goggles, hard hats, uniforms, special shoes and gloves, and smocks.

14) Often-overlooked expenses when you're on a business trip. These include dry cleaning and laundry, telephone calls home, transportation, food, and lodging.

15) Rewards. If you lose your briefcase, luggage, or other business property, you can deduct the cost of advertising for its return, or the dollar amount of the reward you pay to the person who finds it.

16) Your car. If you use your car for business, you can claim the fixed mileage allowance by the IRS, which is currently 22.5 cents per mile for the first 15,000 miles, and 11 cents thereafter. Or, if you feel this falls short of your actual automobile expenses, you can add up your true expenses, including depreciation for wear and tear on the car. If your car is used over 50% of the time for business, you have a choice of writing off a set amount or depreciating its value over several years. Consult an accountant for details.

17) Country club dues. A proportionate amount of your dues is an acceptable deduction to the IRS if you use your club for business more than half the time.

18) Commuting costs. If you have more than one job, you can deduct the cost of commuting. The cost of travel *between* the two jobsites is deductible, but not from home to work and back again.

19) Home-entertaining costs. The cost of entertaining business clients at home is 80% deductible provided business discussions take place.

20) $25 per person for business gifts. Business gifts to customers and clients are deductible up to this amount.

15 If You Are an Employee

This category has only a few tax breaks left since the passage of the 1986 Tax Reform Act. In fact, nearly everything you receive in payment for your services is now taxed. The rare exceptions are described below.

1) Get a Social Security refund. Check to see if you overpaid your Social Security tax. This is most likely to happen if you have more than one employer. The limit you should have paid in 1988 is $3,380.

2) Make a loan to your employer. Ask your employer to reimburse you for out-of-pocket business expenses rather than give you an allowance. If you were on an allowance, you'd only be allowed to deduct those expenses that are unreimbursed; you'd have to itemize, and then meet the 2% floor for miscellaneous expenses. And to meet the 2% floor, you could only use 80% of your unreimbursed meal and entertainment expenses. But if you pay for entertainment or other expenses out of your own pocket—that is, if the costs are not advanced to you, but rather, you advanced the money to your employer—all those unreimbursed expenses can be taken as adjustments to your income, which are better than itemized deductions.

3) Deduct business expenses. If you are not reimbursed for any business expenses you incur, you can claim 80% of them on Schedule A as itemized miscellaneous deductions, subject to the 2% floor.

4) Deduct job-hunting expenses. These are subject to the 2% floor. People often forget to include visits to employment agencies, phone calls to potential employers, postage and envelopes for mailing résumés, photocopies of job-search items, and interview travel costs. For any of these to be deductible, you must be looking for work in the same field you are in now. You can deduct 22.5 cents per mile, tolls, and parking (but not gas) if you drive to an interview. If you take public transportation you can deduct the exact amount.

5) Claim a home office. If you and your employer agree that you can or should work at home—even part of the time— consider setting up a separate home office (see also pages 82–83).

6) Deduct fun. If you are not reimbursed for entertainment expenses, 80% of the cost of wining, dining, and entertaining clients is deductible, subject to the 2% floor for miscellaneous deductions.

7) If your employer reimbursed you or directly picked up the tab for expenses attendant to your job-related move, these costs are reportable as income but can be taken as miscellaneous itemized deductions on Schedule A, without regard to the 2% floor.

8) Deduct commuting costs. If you have more than one job, the expense of travel *between* the two jobsites is deductible, but not from home to work or back again.

16 If You Are a Parent

Being a parent these days is an expensive affair, but the IRS provides several worthwhile tax savers to ease the burden. If you can take advantage of at least one of the following suggestions, you will ease the financial burden you carry.

1) Take the child-care tax credit (see pages 72–74) if you work, are looking for work, are disabled, or are a part-time student.

2) Shift income to your children. The first $500 of a dependent child's investment (or unearned) income is tax free if the child is under age 14. This includes interest and dividend income as well as capital gains. The next $500 is taxed at the child's rate, which is almost always in the lowest bracket of 15%. By transferring some of your income-producing assets to your child, you will reduce your taxes—provided you keep the income earned under $1,000 per year. If the income is over $1,000, then it is generally taxed at the parent's rate until the child turns 14, when it is all taxed at the child's rate.

The question often arises: "When it's taxed at the parent's rate, which parent?" If the parents are divorced or legally separated, the rate is that of the custodial parent. If the parents are married and file separate tax returns, the rate is that of the parent with the greater income.

3) Use EE Savings Bonds. If your child has a low income, have him or her report the annual interest on EE bonds he or she owns, rather than deferring the interest until the bonds are redeemed. By reporting each year's accumulation, up to $500 per year will permanently escape taxation. Interest tables are found in the Savings Bond Redemption Chart available from most local banks and all Federal Reserve Banks.

4) Hire your children. If you are self-employed, operate a business, or do part-time free-lance work, hire your children. The tax advantage is that you can deduct their wages, thereby reducing your business taxable income. It also keeps the money in the family. And if your dependent child earns less than $3,000 in 1988, none of it will be taxed, so in effect you are shifting $3,000 tax-free from your business into your family coffers. If your child is under 21, you are not required to pay Social Security taxes on his or her wages. To pass IRS scrutiny, the pay must be fair and reasonable and the work real, such as answering phones, typing, filing, or doing library research.

5) Open an IRA. Your child can use the money he or she earns to start funding an IRA. Although this is not to *your* advantage, it is to his or hers. The investment, and the interest it earns, can accumulate tax free for perhaps as long as 50 years.

6) Get a tax credit of up to $851 or more. In 1987, if your income was less than $15,432, you had a dependent child, and you met certain other requirements, you were entitled to an earned income tax credit of as much as $851 (see page 74). For 1988, your adjusted gross income cannot exceed $17,000 in order to qualify; the maximum credit is adjusted at the end of each year for inflation.

7) Seek out extra medical deductions. Some special-education expenses for the physically and mentally handicapped are deductible as medical expenses, especially if they are documented. Ask your child's school to write a letter specifying the dollar amount of its bills that are medically related.

8) Give away up to $10,000 and reduce your taxable income. You may give up to $10,000 a year ($20,000 for joint gifts) to other members of your family, tax free. And, if this money goes to your child or someone else in a lower tax bracket, it will be taxed at his or her lower rate. In the meantime, you have less taxable income to report.

9) Build a college fund for your child. Give yourself some tax advantages and at the same time build a college tuition kitty with investments in your child's name. Until your child is 14 (at which time he or she is taxed as an adult) invest in tax-exempt municipal bonds, zero coupon bonds, EE savings bonds, or single-premium annuities or life insurance. When your child turns 14 and begins to pay his or her own taxes on investments, you may wish to switch to higher-income-producing stocks and bonds.

17 If You Save or Invest

By carefully selecting your investments and timing their purchase and sale or redemption, you can significantly reduce your tax bite. If you are already actively involved in the stock market, your broker will provide additional suggestions. All investors and savers, however, can use the following tax tips.

1) Put off paying taxes on interest until next year. U.S. Treasury bills have maturity times of up to 1 year; although the interest accrues over this time period, it is taxed *only* when it matures. Buy a T-bill or CD due to mature next year in order to postpone taxes. And there's another tax break: T-bill interest is exempt from state taxes in *all* states.

2) Find tax-free interest. A tax-free municipal bond that yields 7% is the equivalent of an 8.2% taxable bond if you are in the 15% tax bracket, and a 9.7% bond if you are in the 28% bracket.

3) Build up your IRA faster. The key advantage to an IRA is the buildup of tax-free interest until the time you start to take money out. Therefore, make your contribution as early in the year as possible. (You have until April 15, 1989, to make your 1988 contribution, for example). If your money is sitting in your regular savings account or money market fund, it is earning taxable interest, so put it in your IRA instead. Remember, you can make a series of small contributions all year long—you don't have to wait until you've accumulated the full $2,000.

4) Don't pay a penalty on premature IRA withdrawals. If you withdraw the money as an annuity based on your life expectancy, or if you are disabled, there is no penalty.

5) Don't report interest earned on your IRA. The IRS says an amazing number of people forget each year and report this item as taxable income.

90

6) Borrow money at little or no interest. With a single-premium life insurance plan you can borrow up to 90% of the cash value of your policy at very low rates. With some policies you can also withdraw the interest earned without having to repay it, and without having to pay income tax on the amount of interest you "borrow."

7) Deduct any CD penalty you paid for cashing in your certificate early. Many savers forget this deduction, which reduces their adjusted gross income.

8) Deduct worthless stocks or bonds. If a stock you own is worthless, you can deduct its cost basis. However, you must prove that it became worthless during the tax year by getting a statement to that effect from your broker or by presenting other evidence that the company went bankrupt or ceased to operate.

9) Use your losses. You can offset capital gains against capital losses. Up to $3,000 of the excess losses over gains can also be used to offset ordinary income. If you have more than $3,000 worth of excess losses, they can be carried over to the next year.

10) Defer income into next year. If you are self-employed, defer billing clients and collecting income. Or, if you are an employee, ask your employer to defer your bonus until next year. Another reason for postponing income: your tax bracket could conceivably be lower next year. (Deferring also gives you a year to invest or spend the money you would have earmarked for paying the tax.)

11) Deduct investment-club expenses. Those expenditures you personally make to help operate an investment club are deductible unless they are made in connection with the earning of tax-exempt income.

12) Deduct insurance. If you lose a stock or bond certificate and you have to post an indemnity bond, deduct the cost of the indemnity bond.

13) Pick the best time to buy a mutual fund. If you buy shares just before the fund distributes capital gains, dividends, or interest income, you will be paying taxes on this distribution even though you didn't own the shares for the full quarter. Call the fund to find out when the dividend will be paid and then buy in several days later to avoid being taxed on shares you would own for only a short time.

14) Buy single-state municipal bonds. If you live in a

91

high-income-tax state, buy single-state tax-free municipals of the state in which you live. They are not only free from federal tax but also from state and local taxes for residents of the state in which the bond is issued. Among the high-income-tax states are New York, California, Minnesota, Maryland, and Ohio.

15) Buy bonds issued by Puerto Rico and the District of Columbia. These municipals are exempt from state, local, and federal taxes for residents of *all* states in the U.S.

16) Don't report interest on accounts that have been frozen, or accounts at insolvent financial institutions. This money is not taxable since it cannot be withdrawn. You will receive notification of such an event from the institution or the bank that is taking over the troubled bank's accounts.

17) Capitalize your brokerage commission. When you calculate your tax gains and losses on securities, include brokerage commissions. When you sell, commissions are subtracted from the sale price, cutting the size of your gain (or increasing the size of your loss). Either way you look at it, your taxes are less.

18) Claim all possible deductions. A number of expenses related to the cost of saving and investing money are deductible. They fall under the category of "miscellaneous itemized deductions" subject to the 2% floor. They include:

- Fees to set up an IRA or Keogh plan;
- Annual custodial charges on an IRA or Keogh (be certain to pay the cost of both fees and custodial charges separately from your IRA or Keogh contribution in order to document this item for the IRS);
- Safety-deposit box costs, if the box is used to house income-producing securities;
- Cost of this book and other investment guides, magazines, or tax publications;
- Investment advisory fees;
- Tax consultants and preparers;
- Telephone calls and postage related to investing.

19) Tax-exempt money market funds. If you wish to reduce your taxable dividend income, use a tax-exempt money market fund for parking your extra cash. Interest rates are lower than those paid on taxable money market funds, but the tax savings may make it worth your while.

92

INCOME THAT IS TAX-FREE

- Cash-value buildup of life insurance policies and deferred annuities
- Life insurance proceeds you receive as a beneficiary
- Employer-made contributions to qualified retirement plans
- Vacation-home-rental income if property is rented out for 14 days or less
- Scholarships and fellowships when used for tuition and course equipment
- Municipal bond interest income
- Tax-exempt money market fund dividends

18 Retirement

Once you reach retirement you may have less money, but far more time during which to spend it. Living successfully on a set income requires sound financial planning, both before *and* after actual retirement. While this kind of money management does have complexities all its own, the following tax-saving ideas are well worth investigating.

1) Take the tax credit for the elderly. If you are 65 or older, or if you are under 65, totally disabled, and receiving disability income, you qualify for this credit. Details are given on page 74.

2) Sign up for your Social Security benefits. They will not be sent to you automatically. To register, visit your local Social Security office at least 3 months before your 65th birthday. Even if you are not planning to retire at 65, register to ensure your Medicare coverage.

3) Understand the Social Security rules. These regulations are continually revised, so it's important to keep up to date in order to make the wisest decisions:

- If you retire before age 65, you can elect to take reduced Social Security benefits starting at age 62.
- If you do not retire at age 65, your potential benefits increase for each year you wait.
- If you are under age 70, Social Security benefits are cut back by any income you earn from employment. The ceiling on this cutback is adjusted for inflation; your Social Security office will provide current figures.
- If you are over age 70, your benefits will not be reduced by income you earn from a job. In fact, you can earn any amount and still receive your full benefits. But remember—if you work you pay Social Security taxes on what you earn, no matter what age you may be.

4) If you are under age 59½ and you want to withdraw money from a qualified retirement plan, IRA, or tax-sheltered annuity, you can avoid the 10% withdrawal penalty if you:

- Arrange for your distributions to be made in the form of a series of approximately equal periodic payments. Once you elect this method, you must continue until age 59½, or for 5 years, whichever is later.
- Satisfy your plan's early retirement provisions (this does not apply to IRA's).
- You have certain medical expenses (check with a tax planner).

5) If you received a lump-sum distribution from your pension or profit-sharing plan, roll it over into an IRA within 60 days and you will not have to pay income tax on the distribution. You may roll over all or part of the distribution, but the dollars not rolled over will be taxed and, if you are under 59½, subject to a 10% penalty. (See pages 40–43.)

6) If you are still contributing to an IRA after December 31 of the tax year, you have until April 15 of the following year to put your contribution into the account and still claim the deduction, provided, of course, you qualify for the IRA. If depositing $2,000 (or whatever you plan to contribute) at any one time is more difficult, pay it in several installments over the course of the 15½ months, or consider making a smaller contribution.

CHECK YOUR SOCIAL SECURITY RECORDS

It's important to check on your earnings as they are recorded at the Social Security Administration, since it has been criticized for not being up to date and for making mistakes. No matter how old you are, once every three years you should mail in Form SSA-7004, "Request for Statement of Earnings," to:

> Social Security Administration
> Data Operations Center
> P.O. Box 20
> Wilkes Barre, PA 18703

You can get this form at your local Social Security office or by calling 800-937-2000.

After you receive the Social Security Administration's statement of your earnings, check it against your own earnings records and W-2's. When writing, you might also want to request free copies of the Administration's booklets, "Estimating Your Social Security Retirement Check" and "Thinking About Retirement."

If you are 55 or older, it is time to ask your local Social Security office to provide an estimate of your retirement benefits.

---

19 Your Tax Future

Now that you've mastered the basics of filing this year's tax return, it's a good idea to start thinking about next year and the years thereafter. Both your personal income and the tax regulations are likely to change in the future. You can cope with these changes most effectively if you are well informed, so be on the lookout for tax-related articles in newspapers and magazines. Clip and read any that you feel pertain to your personal situation and stash them in your file, ready to review when you prepare your next return. Two key areas to look for are changes in the tax brackets and any new rulings pertaining to IRA's, Keoghs, or other retirement plans.

With luck and hard work, your income will rise next year or shortly thereafter. This, too, will necessitate modification of how you invest, as well as how you handle your taxes. If you move from the 15% to the 28% tax bracket, for instance, you should consider ways to shelter some or all of your new income from the long arm of the IRS. Municipal bonds and tax-free money market funds should be your first line of defense. You may also wish to investigate two special types of limited partnerships that have tax benefits for those in the higher bracket: low-income housing and real estate rehabilitation projects.

Regardless of what other things the future holds for you, taxes are here to stay. But if you are armed with enough information and know-how, you can astutely handle any new regulations handed down by Congress.

Appendix

Getting Help with Your Return

Preparing your tax return can be detailed work, especially if you itemize. And, the 1986 Tax Reform Act—which jettisoned many of the old rules and replaced them with a rash of new ones—has complicated the task. It's not surprising, then, that millions of Americans seek help in preparing their returns.

Do you need help? The answer is probably "yes" if:

- You had a major change in your life during the year—such as marriage, divorce, death of a parent or spouse, or retirement.
- You made a major purchase—such as a house, land, or a business.
- You are self-employed.
- You were extremely active in the stock market.
- You received income from sources other than your job.
- You inherited money or property.
- You hate number-crunching.

How to Pick the Best

Before you select an income tax preparer, you must decide what type of service you need and how much you want to pay. As a general rule, the more complex your situation, the more specialized the advice you require.

Do your research carefully, just as you would for finding a doctor or lawyer. Ask friends and colleagues for referrals, or go to professional organizations for recommendations. Then interview the preparer, preferably in person. Among the questions to ask the potential preparer are:

1) **What are your qualifications and training?** You want someone whose practice includes people in your financial category and who is familiar with any particular problems you may have. If you are a free-lancer, for example, you need a preparer who knows that particular element of the tax code.

2) **How much do you charge?** Does the fee include only filling out the return, or planning sessions as well? Is it an hourly rate, or a flat rate?

3) **Will you be the person actually doing my return, and will you represent me if I'm audited?**

4) **How many forms do you prepare each year?**

5) **Will your work be reviewed by anyone else for accuracy?**

Nationwide Tax Services (Storefront Chains)

These large firms, with operations in most cities and towns, are geared toward helping a specific type of taxpayer—those with routine returns or only slightly complicated problems. Most will review your completed return for free, and then, if they discover an error or can improve on your return, will charge for advice.

A key advantage is price: The largest of these chains, H & R Block, for instance, charges an average of $44 for doing a routine return. Its employees, and those of other similar firms, are required to take a 75-hour seminar given by their company, and then to pass an examination based on the seminar. If possible, interview preparers at these firms, selecting one whom you like. Make certain, however, that the person will represent you if you are audited, and that the firm will pay any interest or penalties you are charged later on due to the preparer's computational errors.

If you require assistance for something other than just filling in the blanks, you may want more sophisticated help from an accountant, enrolled agent, certified public accountant, or tax attorney. These professionals are available year-round, whereas many of the individual storefront tax preparers work seasonally.

Note: Tax preparers cannot divulge any personal or financial information you provide them, except under court order. The maximum penalty for violation is 1 year in jail and a $1,000 fine.

Public Accountants

Accountants must have a bachelor's degree and work in the practice of accountancy. Many are "enrolled agents" (see below), but since there are no formal educational requirements or tests to pass for an accountant to open shop, make certain any accountant you use is experienced in doing tax returns, is a member of his or her state professional accountants' organization, and is enrolled in a continuing-education program. Fees are approximately the same as those of enrolled agents, and there are many more public accountants than enrolled agents, so if your return is relatively simple a public accountant will be able to prepare it for you.

Enrolled Agents

"EA's," as they are called, in addition to preparing tax returns, are approved by the IRS to represent taxpayers before the IRS. There are over 30,000 EA's practicing as independent consultants or with firms. They are well versed in tax law. To qualify, an EA must pass an IRS-administered comprehensive exam; and to maintain accreditation, he or she must complete a minimum number of hours in an annual continuing-education program. Their fees start at around $150 for a relatively uncomplicated form. To find an EA in your area, contact:

> The National Association of Enrolled Agents
> 6000 Executive Blvd.
> Rockville, MD 20952
> 800-424-4339

Certified Public Accountants

CPA's have more training than accountants. They, too, have a college degree, but have also passed a state professional exam, and have had at least 2 years of auditing experience. Although CPA's are extremely skilled in accounting, not all are tax experts. If you use a CPA, make certain he or she has expertise in the tax area and is enrolled in a continuing-education program to keep up to date on the new tax laws. Fees vary depending upon where you live—typically starting at $75 an hour—but many charge much more. Call the Association of Certified Public Accountants in your state for a list of members.

Tax Attorneys

These professionals are the top specialists in the field. Their expertise includes estate planning, tax shelters, municipal bonds, and other matters generally related to wealthy taxpayers. Their fees are also tops, so until your income is equally high, it's probably safe to save your money and use a less-pricey pro.

Getting the Best

You can help get the best from your tax preparer and save on his or her bill by taking the following four steps:

1) Be knowledgeable about the tax laws yourself. By reading this book as well as current IRS publications, you will understand the basic concepts and know what material your tax preparer will need from you.

2) Organize your records. Don't walk in with a shoebox full of torn receipts and pieces of paper. You'll be charged for the time it takes to sort out your files, and it's likely you will overlook important papers. Get everything in shape ahead of time.

3) Bring the right materials. Among the items you should take to your meeting are previous tax returns; your tax statements, such as your W-2 form and all 1099 forms; an expense log, if you have kept one; all canceled checks for the year, categorized by topic; and completed worksheets, either those sent to you by the tax preparer or those found in this book.

4) Begin early. You should receive your W-2's and 1099's by February 1, so call for your appointment as soon as possible after the start of the new year. Don't wait until a week before April 15 and expect to get good service. As the tax seasons draws to a close, preparers are extremely rushed, and your tax return might suffer.

AVOID A TAX PREPARER WHO:

- Promises you a refund before looking at your return;
- Asks you to sign a blank return;
- Asks you to sign a return that is done in pencil;
- Has no suggestions and merely fills out your form;
- Is too busy or uninterested to answer your questions.

Amending Your Return

If you find a mistake on a past income tax return—or you discover that you could have paid less tax—you can address either situation by filing an amended return. It's worth doing if you'll get a refund and if you are confident that your original return will survive an audit. (Not all amended returns are audited, by any means, but amending may trigger the IRS to take a closer look.)

You have 3 years from the time you filed your return to amend it, or within 2 years from the time you paid the tax, whichever is later. (If you filed no return, you have two years from the time the tax was paid.) The IRS pays interest on money it refunds as the result of an amended return; the current interest rate on refunded overpayments is 9%. If you filed Form 1040, 1040A, or 1040EZ, use Form 1040X, "Amended U.S. Individual Income Tax Return," to file an amended return.

Tracking Down a Missing Refund

If you do not receive your refund within 10 weeks after filing, you can check up on it by calling the Automated Refund Information System number, which in many areas of the country is 800-544-4477. The instructions attached to your IRS Form 1040, 1040A, and 1040EZ give the number for the area in which you live.

When you call, have the following information at hand: your filing status, the first (or only) Social Security number listed on the return, the amount of refund you expect, and the year for which the refund was due.

If you do not get satisfactory action from the Automated Refund Information System, call—or, better yet, write to—the IRS service center in your area. Be sure to keep a copy of your letter.

How Taxes Are Collected

Our tax system requires that you make tax payments as you earn your income. This can be accomplished in two ways: Tax can be withheld from your wages and salary; or, if you receive income not subject to withholding, you must file quarterly estimated tax returns and pay a portion of that tax with each estimate. If you fail to pay by withholding or by "quarterlies," you will face a penalty for underpayment.

Withholding

Each pay period, your employer withholds tax from your gross salary and sends that money to the government. The amount withheld depends upon your marital status and the number of exemptions you claim. You must file a withholding certificate (Form W-4) with your employer, indicating your filing status and number of exemptions, by October 1.

By January 31, your employer must give you Copy B of Form W-2, the record of your pay and what has been withheld. Your W-2 will also list withheld Social Security taxes (sometimes identified as F.I.C.A., which stands for Federal Insurance Contributions Act). Your W-2 must be filed with your tax return.

Estimated Tax Payments

The second way to pay taxes on time is through quarterly filings of estimated tax returns. These are required if you are not subject to withholding—for example, if you are self-employed or receive only investment income—or if the withholding from your wages is not enough to cover your tax liability.

Estimated taxes are due on April 15, June 15, September 15, and January 15. With each return you should submit 25% of the required total payment for the year. Payments must equal the lesser of 100% of your previous year's taxes or 90% of your current year's liability. (It is probably easier to pay on the basis of last year's tax than it is to make an accurate estimate of the new year's income.) Estimated payments are indicated on Line 55 on your Form 1040.

Signing Your Return

You must sign *and* date your return. If you are filing a joint return, both you and your spouse must sign and date it. Children who are old enough to write can sign their own return if they are obligated to file. For those too young to write, a parent may sign the child's name. If you paid someone to prepare your return, the preparer must sign and include his or her Social Security number. If the tax preparer works at a firm, the firm's name, address, and tax identification number must be included as well.

Getting an Extension

If you cannot file your return on time, you can get an automatic 4-month extension by filling Form 4868, "Application for Automatic Extension of Time to File U.S. Individual Income Tax Return." It must be filed by April 15. You do not need to give any special reason, as this extension is available to everyone.

If at the end of the 4-month automatic extension you still need more time, you can request 2 more months by filing Form 2688, "Application for Additional Extension of Time to File." In this case you must give a valid reason, such as that you have not received information necessary to complete your form. Illness in the family or loss of records due to fire, for example, are usually acceptable reasons. However, such excuses as "I was too busy" or "My accountant got sick" won't work.

Paying the IRS

No matter how difficult it is, try to pay Uncle Sam on time—by April 15, or quarterly, whichever applies. Failure to do so is injurious to your pocketbook: The IRS charges exorbitant rates on overdue taxes—10% annual interest, *plus* a penalty on the unpaid balance that begins at one-half of 1% per month and rises one-half a percentage point each month, up to 25%.

If You Need to Raise Cash

If you had too little tax withheld from your paycheck last year, if you haven't saved any money from your self-employed wages to pay your quarterly estimated payments, or if you're hit with an unexpected bill from the IRS, you'll need to raise cash, and in a hurry. Stiff IRS penalties may actually make it worth your while to borrow in order to pay your taxes. Following is a list of 8 places to find cash, quickly and conveniently. Compare the various interest rates, and keep in mind that many charge almost as much as the IRS.

• **Your bank.** If you have overdraft privileges with your checking account, you may be able to get cash immediately. Find out if the amount is restricted and what the interest rate is. If you've been a steady customer, you may also be able to take out an unsecured personal loan at your bank.

- **Your credit card.** Most credit cards will advance cash, but at extremely high rates. Use this method only if you must, or while you're waiting for other money to come through.

- **Your credit union.** At credit unions, rates on personal loans and against savings accounts tend to be lower than those at commercial banks. If you are lucky enough to belong to one, a credit union is one of the better sources of quick cash.

- **Your investments.** You can sell stocks or bonds to raise cash, or you can turn in a CD prematurely and pay the penalty. If you have a margin account with a brokerage firm, you can borrow against it within a matter of days. Again, check the rates.

- **Your employer.** Some company savings plans allow employees to borrow up to a certain dollar amount, or half their vested amount. Rates, amounts, and terms vary. Check with your personnel officer.

- **Your life insurance.** Check your policy; you can generally borrow the cash value from all types of life insurance at relatively low rates.

- **Your house.** If you're really pressed you can turn to a home equity loan on your house. These loans, however, are expensive, and rates vary widely. Find out about all the fees they carry, as well as any other costs, before signing on the dotted line.

- **Your family and friends.** You may be able to borrow at little or no interest from those who know you. But if you do, keep the matter strictly business: Fill out a regular promissory note, available at stationery stores, and repay according to your agreement.

If You Absolutely Cannot Pay

If you still cannot come up with the money in time, follow these steps:

1) **File your return anyway.** The worst thing you can do is

not file a return—in fact, it is technically a criminal act. Owing money, however, is not a crime.

2) Pay as much as you can when you file your return.

3) Wait for the IRS to bill you for the unpaid amount, usually in 6 to 8 weeks after you have filed. If you still don't have the money to pay when you get your bill, set up a meeting at your local IRS office. You may be able to arrange to pay your debt over time if you can prove you don't have assets that can be sold. Bring with you an analysis of your monthly income and expenses. In general, the IRS tries to work with people who show they want to make a serious attempt to pay their taxes.

What's on File at the IRS

Long before you file your return, the IRS collects information on you—from your employers, for example—and matches this information with what you report. Should you fail to provide income data that has already been reported to the IRS, you will face a negligence penalty. Here's what the IRS already knows about you.

• **Your wages.** The IRS knows how much money you have earned in wages because your employer sends them a copy of your W-2 Form. This includes regular income, bonuses, vacation and travel allowances, severance pay, and moving-expense payments.

• **Your income.** People who paid you during the year in a form other than wages must report these payments to the IRS on Form 1099-MISC, "Statement for Recipients of Miscellaneous Income." This includes free-lance income, rent or royalty payments, and prizes and awards.

• **Interest income.** Banks and financial institutions report any interest you earn to the IRS on Form 1099-INT, "Statement for Recipients of Interest Income."

• **Tax-refund income.** State and local governments report refund payments of more than $10 on Form 1099-G, "Statement for Recipients of Certain Government Payments."

• **Gambling winnings.** If you win money legally from jai alai, lotteries, raffles, Bingo, slot machines, Keno, horse and dog racing, or the like, the IRS knows about it. It is reported on Form W-2G, "Statement for Recipients of Certain Gambling Winnings."

• **Other income.** The IRS also knows about mortgage interest you received from individuals to whom you made a loan; money received from your brokerage account; information on barter exchanges; distributions from IRA's, Keoghs, and pension plans; cash payments of over $10,000 received from any business transaction; fringe benefits received from your employer; your Social Security benefits; and any unemployment income you have received.

If You Are Audited

Should you be audited by the IRS, keep in mind that only enrolled agents, certified public accountants, and tax attorneys are authorized to represent you before the IRS. According to law, any person who is paid to prepare your tax return *must* appear as a witness and give testimony, if requested to do so by the IRS.

Many national tax services advertise that they will go with you to the IRS, and they actually will. However, they might only show how they arrived at the figures on your return, and not truly argue in your behalf. That's why it's advisable to find out precisely how much help a tax preparer will give you before you hire him or her.

How to Get Ready for an Audit

You will be notified of an audit by an official IRS audit letter. Do not panic, and do not ignore the letter; once the IRS has set its wheels in motion, you have no choice but to see things through to the end. It's easy to feel intimidated by the IRS, but remember that this is an opportunity for you to verify that your tax return is accurate. Take the following steps to prepare for your audit:

1) Call your tax preparer and schedule a meeting to review your return as soon as possible. It's critical that you meet with him or her *before* your meeting with the IRS. Be sure to bring to this meeting all your tax materials for the tax year in question, as well as any supportive documents you may have relating to the particular issues the IRS has identified in its letter. If the IRS wants to review your charitable contributions, for example, bring all your receipts, appraiser's statements, and canceled checks relating to those contributions.

2) Have your tax preparer schedule the meeting with the IRS. He or she is used to dealing with them, and by acting on your behalf will help to establish the correct professional atmosphere. The IRS, however, dictates the setting of your meeting. Although they may permit a simple audit to be conducted by mail (*never* send the IRS anything without keeping a copy!), it is far more likely that they will want the meeting to take place either at your accountant's office or at their office.

3) Regardless of where you meet, there are several things you should be sure to do:

- Arrive on time.
- Dress conservatively and don't wear a lot of flashy jewelry; you want to appear businesslike, not arrogant or cocky.
- Answer all questions directly, but do not volunteer additional information—you could end up talking yourself into a corner.

The Final Word

Your meeting will probably conclude when the auditor has finished questioning you. Occasionally an auditor will give you a decision on the spot, but it is more likely that you will receive a decision by mail, usually in a couple of weeks (depending on the time of year and how busy the IRS is). Because the auditor may ask you to leave some of your papers behind, be sure to make copies of everything beforehand. On rare occasions a taxpayer may be called back for a second meeting, particularly if tax shelters are at issue.

Although many people wind up paying a small amount of additional tax as the result of their audit, the good news is that recent statistics show one out of six audited taxpayers receives a refund.

Keeping Good Records

One easy way to ensure that you pay the least tax you owe is by providing thorough documentation of your expenses and sources of income. These records not only support your deduction claims, but they also make it a great deal easier to fill out your tax return accurately and on time. And, if you use a professional tax preparer, well-organized files will save you money since most preparers charge by the hour.

But don't wait until April 1 to start frantically gathering together every scrap of paper you need. Instead, set up an ongoing system for storing pertinent records *today*—one that you can use easily all year long, such as a drawer in a filing cabinet or a simple accordion folder. Use the following checklist as your guide, and resolve to bring your files up to date every 3 months.

Items to Keep
- Canceled checks
- Business-related receipts showing amount paid, to whom, and for what reason
- Previous tax returns
- Social Security numbers
- Birth certificates

For each of the following categories, keep all receipts and canceled checks:

Records Pertaining to Your Exemptions
- If you are a divorced parent, keep Form 8332 indicating which parent claims the exemption, if it is required;
- Your children's birth certificates and Social Security numbers;
- Your birth certificate, especially if you are over age 65;
- Physician's documentation if you are legally blind or disabled.

Records Pertaining to Your Income
- For wages: Form W-2; generally mailed out by your employer by January 31;
- For tips: Journal recording tips received, from whom, date, amount; or use Form 4070-A;
- For interest income: Form 1099-INT or Form 1099-D; bank statements;
- For dividend income: Form 1099-DIV;
- For refund of state and local taxes: Form 1099-G;
- For paying or receiving alimony: deposit slips, bank statements, divorce papers, ex-spouse's Social Security number;
- For business income: Form 1099-MISC; bank statements, invoices, receipts;
- For investment income: Form 1099-B and copies of brokerage confirmation slips and statements;
- For renting property: Journal indicating number of days

property was rented, number of days personally used; receipts for expenses; log of travel to and from property; rental contracts;
- For unemployment compensation: Form 1099-G;
- For Social Security income: Form 1099-SSA;
- For gambling income: Form W-2G, Form 1099; journal of daily winnings and losses, including losing tickets.

Records Pertaining to Your Adjustments to Income
- If you were penalized for an early withdrawal of savings: Form 1099-INT;
- Copy of pension plan, IRA, or Keogh documentation; statement of contribution by trustee.

Records Pertaining to Your Deductions Made on Schedule A
- For medical deductions: Doctors' bills, prescription statements, log of travel and lodging costs;
- Mortgage statements from bank or mortgager; mortgage contract and documents reported on Form 1098;
- Credit card year-end statement showing interest paid for the year;
- For charitable donations: Statement from charity, including name, address, and amount of donation;
- For casualty and theft losses: Police and insurance reports, bills documenting repairs and replacement of items;
- If you use your car for business: Documentation of the cost of the car, preferably the original purchase document; statement from employer indicating why you are required to use the car; receipts for maintenance and repairs, tolls, parking, gasoline, etc.; a log of expenses that includes date, mileage, and destination;
- If you travel for business: Daily log that includes costs, dates, destination, and reason for trip; credit card slips and receipts;
- For meals and entertainment: Daily log that includes cost of meal or entertainment, location, guest, purpose, date, business discussed, receipts or credit card slips;
- For moving expenses: Canceled checks, receipts, and daily log recording expenses.

Records Pertaining to Your Credits

- For child/dependent care: Canceled checks for amounts paid for care;
- For estimated taxes: Previous year's tax return; canceled checks to IRS;
- For disablement: Physician's statement that you are permanently disabled.

The Key Schedules

When filing your tax return, it is often necessary to supplement your 1040 with one of the following Schedules, on which you supply more detailed information about certain deductions, income, etc. The most important Schedules and what they cover are listed below.

Schedule A: Itemized Deductions

If you decide to itemize your deductions, rather than take the standard deduction, you must fill out Schedule A. The main areas in which you might be able to take deductions are medical and dental expenses; state and local income taxes and property taxes previously paid; interest paid, such as mortgage interest; casualty and theft losses; moving expenses; unreimbursed job expenses; gifts to charity; and other expenses.

Schedule B: Interest and Dividends

If you received more than $400 in taxable interest income or dividends, report it on this Schedule.

Schedule C: Profit or Loss from a Business or Profession

Self-employed persons, as well as those who have income from a sideline business such as free-lance work, must fill out Schedule C. Expenses related to such a business can be deducted on Schedule C and are not subject to the 2% floor for miscellaneous deductions.

Schedule D: Capital Gains and Losses

List all sales of stocks, bonds, and securities as reported to you on Form 1099-B. Include real estate transactions reported to you on Form 1099-S under "Other."

Schedule E: Supplemental Income

Rental and royalty income and losses, as well as income from estates and trusts, are listed here.

Schedule F: Farm Income

Profits and losses from farming activities are reported on this Schedule.

Schedule R: Credit for the Elderly and the Disabled

This includes space for a physician's signature verifying the disability of the taxpayer.

Schedule SE: Computation of Social Security Self-Employment Tax

Self-employed persons must pay a 13.02% Social Security tax on the first $45,000 of earned income, even if they are also receiving Social Security benefits.

Helpful IRS Publications

These publications, written for the general public, are available free of charge at your local IRS office, or by calling 800-424-FORM (3676). They provide additional explanations on individual tax topics. For a complete list of all IRS publications, ask for publication #910, "Guide to Free Tax Services."

Worksheets

The worksheets on the following pages have been designed to help you organize some of the most important information about your personal finances. Filling them in now and adding to them throughout the year will help you establish good record-keeping habits, and may even inspire you to create some other customized worksheets of your own. By tax time, you'll have given yourself a distinct advantage: Most of what you'll need to complete your tax return quickly and easily will be right at your fingertips.

Basic Information About You and Your Dependents

Gathering some basic information such as the following about yourself and your dependents is a good way to establish the record-keeping habit. The following information should be updated regularly.

	Birthdate	Soc. Sec. #	Student?	Income
Your Name				
•				
Spouse's Name				
•				

Dependent Children
Name

•

•

•

•

•

•

Other Dependents
Name (Relationship)   Birthdate   Soc. Sec. #   Student?   Income

-
-
-
-
-
-
-
-
-
-

Salary and Wage Income

Each employer for whom you work during the year will send you a W-2 form showing your wages and the amount of income and Social Security taxes that are withheld. If you do not receive your W-2 form from each employer by January 31, contact them.

Your Name _____ **Tax Year 19____**

Employer	Wages	F.I.C.A. Withheld	Federal Taxes Withheld	State Taxes Withheld	City Tax Withheld	Other With- holdings
•						
•						
•						
•						
•						
•						
•						

Spouse's Name _____ **Tax Year 19____**

Employer	Wages	F.I.C.A. Withheld	Federal Taxes Withheld	State Taxes Withheld	City Tax Withheld	Other Withholdings

Passive Income
Taxable Income for Tax Year 19____

Source	Account Number	Amount	Ownership: Joint/ Single, in name of
•			
•			
•			
•			
•			
•			
•			
•			
•			

Tax-exempt Interest for Tax Year 19___

Source	Account Number	Amount	Ownership: Joint/ Single, in name of
•			
•			
•			
•			
•			
•			
•			
•			
•			

Estimated Taxes Paid
Tax Year 19____

Quarter	Federal: Amount Paid	Date Paid	State: Amount Paid	Date Paid	Local: Amount Paid	Date Paid
1st (due 4/15)						
2nd (due 6/15)						
3rd (due 9/15)						
4th (due 1/15)						
Total Paid						

Charitable Contributions
Tax Year 19____

Organization	Date	Amount	Transportation Expenses

Moving Expenses

	Amount
Expenses incurred while looking for new home	
Travel	
Lodging	
Meals (subject to 80% limit)	
Cost of moving household goods	
Expenses traveling to new home	
Travel	
Lodging	
Meals (subject to 80% limit)	
Temporary expenses for up to 30 consecutive days after getting new job	
Lodging	
Meals (subject to 80% limit)	

Amount

Other

Settling an unexpired lease

• • • • • • • • • • •